Angels

Angels

Divine Messengers and Personal Guardians

LEE FABER

Abbeydale Press

Published by Abbeydale Press an imprint of Bookmart Ltd
Registered number 2372865
Trading as Bookmart Ltd
Blaby Road, Wigston, Leicester
LE18 4SE, England

Produced by Omnipress Limited, UK
Cover design by Omnipress Limited, UK

ABOUT THE AUTHOR

Lee Faber is a native-born American who became a British citizen, having been in the UK since 1981. She has lived and worked in New York, Florida, London and now resides in Wiltshire. During her career she has been involved in book editing and writing with an emphasis on health, food and cookery. She has specialised in Americanising/Anglicising books on a variety of subjects for both US and UK publishers. She is also the author of *Healthy Oils, Aloe Vera, Berries, Juices* and *Smoothies* and in another series, *The Beginners Guide to Chickens, Raising Pigs* and *Raising Goats*. Lee is an accomplished cook and has created many recipes.

DISCLAIMER

These ideas are passed on in good faith, but the author does not guarantee results, nor can she be held responsible for any adverse results. Neither the authors nor the publisher can accept any legal responsibility or liability for any errors or omissions that may be made nor for any inaccuracies nor for any harm or injury that comes about from following instructions or advice in this book.

Contents

Introduction

I believe in angels. In my experience people generally fall into three camps – those who believe, those who want to believe and those who don't believe. The first and the third are equally adamant.

WHAT IS AN ANGEL?
Angels are divine messengers and personal guardians. The general belief in both eastern and western religions is that everyone has a guardian angel who protects the person to whom God assigns them and that they present prayers to God on that person's behalf. The idea that God sends a spirit to watch every individual was common in ancient Greek philosophy and Plato alluded to it in *Phaedo*, one of his great dialogues. Throughout history angels have been our connection to heaven.

There appears to be a certain amount of confusion for some people between angels, demons/devils, spirits, ghosts and fairies.

There is some overlap, but this is how I perceive it.

Angel – A usually benevolent celestial being that acts as an intermediary between heaven and earth.

Demon – A malevolent supernatural being – a devil. 'The Devil', on the other hand, is the title given to the supernatural being who in mainstream religion is believed to be a powerful, evil entity and the tempter of mankind.

Ghost – The spirit of a dead person, especially one believed to appear in bodily likeness to living persons or to haunt former habitats.

Fairy – An imaginary being in human form, depicted as clever, mischievous and possessing magical powers.

Spirit – Now here it gets complicated because

a spirit can be what is thought of as the 'soul', considered as departing from the body of a person at death or a supernatural being, such as an angel or demon, or a fairy or sprite. So the word 'spirit' takes in the entire gamut from the intangible real to the imaginary.

HOW DO YOU KNOW WHEN YOU HAVE MET AN ANGEL?

For millennia humans have pondered the nature of angels. One of the most common questions people who have not yet had an angel encounter ask is 'What do angels look like?'

Perhaps because angels are spiritual beings, our eyes cannot see the spirit, so we must create a corporeal being. In the Bible we are taught that angels can move with tremendous speed, so our guardian angels can keep watch over us even if they are such a great distance away that it is impossible to see them.

Based on various Bible passages and stories people have told me, sometimes angels

> We cannot pass our guardian angel's bounds, resigned or sullen, he will hear our sighs.
>
> SAINT AUGUSTINE

appear as people like you and me. Hebrews 13:2 states, 'Be not forgetful to entertain strangers: for thereby some have entertained angels unawares'. This suggests that we may have encountered an angel, but have not realised it. Often, as angels do their work, they remain unseen and we are not aware of their activity.

I believe that angels have the ability to temporarily assume a shape that humans can see when there is a reason for them to do so. Many people who have had angel experiences have sensed an angel's presence as a person surrounded by a glowing brightness, or as an unseen being bathed in light, or even just brilliant light. In Psalm 104:4, angels are described as a flaming fire.

I've had a long relationship with my angel, who, because I needed a vision, rather than just a presence, I have always pictured as female, with long curling dark hair, big blue eyes and fluffy wings, wearing a flowing white gown. Not fashioned in my image then.

People who are spiritually aware are more likely to have angel encounters than disbelievers. A friend told me 'I have felt at two distinct times in my life that I had guardian angels. Once when I was very young (pre-kindergarten, I think) I came close to drowning in a playmate's swimming pool and I felt something or someone pull me to safety. I feel that angels are real, just as I know God and Jesus and the Holy Spirit are real. We can feel them, even if we can't see them.' Sometimes the encounter isn't quite that dramatic. How many times have you lost an important object and search though you might, you cannot find it. Then, when you have almost completely given up hope, it appears, sometimes right under your nose. Someplace you are certain you have already searched. Or you are blithely walking along, not paying a great deal of attention, when you stumble badly, but don't fall and sense that someone has steadied you, helping you avoid injury. Is this divine intervention?

One question that is very often asked is

'Are angels male or female?' Angels throughout history and art have frequently been depicted as beautiful women with magnificent wings, dressed in flowing robes and in Biblical references they frequently take on a male guise. But angels are neither women nor men. They do not have a gender. They are different from people, even if they are sometimes seen in human form.

Angels come in all shapes and sizes; all ages and
*   skin types*
Some with freckles, some with dimples, some
*   with wrinkles, some without*
They come disguised as friends, enemies, teachers,
*   students, lovers and fools.*
They don't take life too seriously, they travel
*   light.*
They leave no forwarding address, they ask
*   nothing in return.*
They wear sneakers with gossamer wings, they
*   get a deal on dry cleaning.*
They are hard to find when your eyes are closed,
But they are everywhere you look, when you
*   choose to see.*   –Anonymous

When I first started writing this book, I thought it was going to be very light-hearted – a meringue if you will as opposed to a dense cheesecake. In fact it has turned into something very different and serious. My typing fingers are being guided, almost as if it (the subject) is writing me.

I have a little angel pin on my baseball cap. It's been there for such a long time, I no longer remember where I got it from or why I felt I needed it there. Perhaps it is to remind me that someone/something is watching out for and protecting me.

ANGELS
IN
RELIGION

Are angels ambassadors sent from God to guide us, to protect us or to bring messages from heaven? If one looks at the Holy Bibles of Christians and Jews, the Qur'an of Islam and the revelations of Zoroaster (Zarathustra) (*c.*628 BC– *c.*551 BC), religious teacher and prophet of ancient Persia, angels fulfil all of these functions.

The word 'angel' is derived from the Greek word *angelos*, which means messenger. It is typically used to describe anyone who brings a message to another, whether a human being or a spirit. The concept of messengers from the spiritual world is one that appears in almost all religions from their beginnings. Within some religions, angels are spirit messengers who bring messages of truth to aid mankind, while fallen angels bring forth messages of untruth to lead people astray and wreak havoc on earth.

In Christian theology, guardian angels are widely believed to be assigned to every person for the duration of their life on earth, providing protection, as well as guidance from the other side. I think it is quite amazing that religions that appear to have completely different beliefs have angels in common.

THE BIBLE
Angels are spirit beings. 'Are they not all ministering spirits, sent forth to minister for them who shall be heirs of salvation?' (Hebrews 1:14), so they do not have any essential physical form. But angels have the ability to take on human form.

In Genesis 18:2-10, God and two angels arrived before Abraham as men 'And he lift up his eyes and looked, and lo, three men stood by him' to announce that his wife Sarah would have a son, which was rather extraordinary as Abraham and Sarah were both elderly.

In Exodus 23:20, God announced: 'Behold, I send an Angel before thee, to keep thee in the way and to bring thee into the place which I have prepared'.

Angels appear as men many times throughout the Bible. At other times, angels appear not as humans, but as something otherworldly. Sometimes their appearance was terrifying to those who encountered them. Often, the first words from these angels were 'do not be afraid', because extreme fear was such a common reaction. Zacharias (Luke 1:12) was speechless with terror before the angel who visited him, as were the keepers of Jesus' tomb, who became as dead men when they saw the angel of the Lord (Matthew 28:4). The shepherds in the fields (Luke 2) were 'sore afraid' when the angel of the Lord appeared and the glory of the Lord shone around them.

To others, angelic appearances did not incur fear at all. Mary's encounter with the angel who announced the birth of Jesus produced confusion at the pronouncement, but didn't seem to produce the fear that Zacharias felt. In terms of physical characteristics, angels are often described as winged. The cherubim on the Ark of the Covenant have wings that cover the mercy seat – the lid of the sacred ark (Exodus 25:20). Isaiah saw winged seraphim in his vision of the throne of heaven, each one having six wings (Isaiah 6:2). Ezekiel also saw visions of winged angels. Isaiah 6:1-2 depicts angels having human features (voices, faces and feet).

Angel voices are heard singing and praising God in several other passages of the Bible. One of the most complete descriptions of an angel is in Daniel 10:5-6. 'I looked up and there before me was a man dressed in linen, with a belt of the finest gold around his waist. His body was like chrysolite, his face like lightning, his eyes like flaming torches, his arms and legs like the gleam of burnished bronze and his voice like the sound of a multitude.'

The angel guarding Jesus' tomb was similarly described. 'His countenance was like lightning and his raiment white as snow' (Matthew 28:3).

Whatever appearance angels assume, there is reason to believe that they are incredibly beautiful. Ezekiel tells us that Lucifer's beauty was such that it caused his heart to be 'lifted up' in pride. Perhaps angels have extraordinary beauty because they are continually in the presence of God, whose glory is reflected upon all that is around Him.

THE QUR'AN

Angels are mentioned frequently in the Holy Qur'an (Koran), which was a revelation to the Prophet Muhammad by the Archangel Gabriel.

Gabriel brought Muhammad two green pieces of cloth from heaven, one of which was decorated with all kinds of precious stones from the earth, and the other with precious elements from heaven.

He opened the first cloth and told the Prophet to sit on it, and he handed him the second one and told him to open it. When he opened it, he received the Holy Qur'an with words of light and the secret of the tree in the seventh heaven was revealed to him.

Whoever reads the Holy Qur'an with sincerity and piety is enabled to enter these oceans of knowledge and light.

The Prophet Muhammad saw a tablet made of rare pearls under the Throne of God and another tablet of emerald. Upon the first was the first chapter, Surat al-Fatiha, which consists of seven verses, and upon the second the entire Qur'an. He asked Gabriel, 'What is the reward of one who reads the Fatiha?' Gabriel said, 'The seven doors of hell will be closed for him, and the seven doors of paradise will be opened for him.'

Muhammad asked, 'What is the reward of the one who recites the whole Qur'an?' Gabriel replied, 'For every letter that he reads God will create an angel that will plant a tree for him in paradise.'
  Then the Prophet saw a triple light radiating in three directions, and he asked what it was. Gabriel said: 'One of them is the light of the Verse of the Throne (2:255), the second is the Chapter Ya Seen (Chapter 36),

and the third is the Chapter of Oneness (Chapter 112)'. He asked, 'What is the reward of one who reads the Verse of the Throne?' Gabriel replied, 'God said it is My attribute, and whoever recites it shall look at Me on Judgment Day without veil.'

The Prophet then asked: 'What is the reward for one who reads the Chapter Ya Seen?' The answer came from God. 'It consists of eighty verses, and whoever reads it will receive eighty mercies: twenty angels will bring him twenty mercies in his life, twenty more angels will bring him twenty mercies at his death, twenty more, twenty mercies in his grave, and twenty others, twenty mercies on Judgment Day.' Muhammad asked: 'What is the reward for reading the Chapter of Oneness?' The answer came: 'The angels will give him to drink from the four heavenly rivers that are mentioned in the Holy Qur'an: the river of pure crystal water, the river of milk, the river of wine, and the river of honey.'

ANGELS IN JUDAISM

The Hebrew word for angel is *malach*, which means messenger.

Angels can appear in a variety of forms, although the Bible often neglects to give any description at all (Judges 6:11-14; Zechariah 4). They are depicted as human in most biblical accounts (Numbers 22) and as such are often indistinguishable from human beings (Genesis 18; 32:10-13; Joshua 5:13-15; Judges 13:1-5) but they also may manifest themselves as pillars of fire and cloud, or as a burning bush. Moses, tending his father-in-law's flock of sheep (Exodus 3), sees a bush burning 'and the Angel of the Lord appeared to him in a flame from the midst of the bush'.

The Psalms characterise natural phenomena, like lightning, as God's melachim (Psalms 104:4): 'Who maketh his angels spirits; his ministers a flaming fire'.

Other divine creatures appear to be winged parts of God's throne. 'Above it stood the seraphim: each one had six wings; with twain he covered his face, and with twain he covered his feet, and with twain he did fly' (Isaiah 6). The appearance of cherubim is well known enough to be artistically rendered on the Ark of the Covenant (Exodus 25).

Biblical angels fulfil a variety of functions, including conveying information to mortals, shielding, rescuing and caring for Israelites and smiting Israel's enemies.

ZOROASTRIANISM

Zoroastrianism recognises various classes of spiritual beings besides the Supreme Being (Ahura Mazda): The Amesha Spentas, Yazatas and Fravashis. In practice, Zoroastrians pick a patron angel for their protection and throughout their lives are careful to observe prayers dedicated to that angel.

Amesha Spentas (Archangels)

Amahraspand, sometimes referred to as Archangels literally, 'Beneficent Immortals', these are the highest spiritual beings created by Ahura Mazda. There are seven Archangels. Their names are: Ameretat (Living), personification of immortality and the protector of plants; Spenta Armaiti (Holy Devotion), presiding over the earth and goddess of fertility; Asha Vahishta (Excellent Order), personification of 'best truth' and protector of physical and moral order on earth; Khshathra Vairya (Desirable Dominion), associated with metals and presiding over the poor; Haurvatat (Personification of Perfection), associated with life after death; Sraosa (Personification of Obedience), the messenger of Ahura Mazda and also guide for the souls of the dead to find their way to the afterlife; Vohu Manah (Good Sense), the personification of wisdom and protector of the animal world, especially cattle.

Fravashis (Guardian Angels)

They are also known as Arda Fravash (Holy Guardian Angels). Each person is accompanied by a guardian angel that acts as a guide throughout life. They originally patrolled the boundaries of the ramparts of

Around our pillows
golden ladders rise,
And up and down
the skies,
With winged sandals
shod,
The angels come and go,
The messengers of God!

RH STODDARD

heaven, but volunteer to descend to earth to stand by individuals to the end of their days. Ahura Mazda advises the Prophet Zarathustra to invoke them for help whenever he finds himself in danger. If not for their guardianship, animals and people could not have continued to exist, because the wicked Druj would have destroyed them all.

The Fravashi also serve as an ideal which the soul has to strive for and emulate and ultimately become one with after death. They manifest the energy of God, and preserve order in the creation. They are said to fly like birds, and are represented by a winged disk, often with a person superimposed.

Yazatas (Angels)

Literally 'adorable ones', a created spiritual being, worthy of being honoured or praised. Like the Amesha Spentas, they personify abstract ideas and virtues, or concrete objects of nature. The Yazatas always try to help people and protect us from evil. There are many Yazatas, each having specific duties.

Angels are found within three key religions: Judaism, Christianity and Islam, plus Zoroastrianism as discussed on the previous page. Yet, angels, or divine helpers, were also found within Sumerian, Babylonian, Egyptian and Greek writings and played a major role in the ideas regarding angels within those religions. For example, it is well known that ancient Sumerian texts pre-dated the Hebrew book of Genesis, including the idea of the existence of angels. The Hebrew beliefs regarding angels were similarly shared with Christianity, and both their teachings of angels inspired Islamic beliefs.

BUDDHISM

The Buddhist equivalent of angels is devas, or celestial beings. Some schools of Buddhism also refer to dharmapalas or dharma protectors. In Tibetan Buddhism, for instance, devas are sometimes considered to be emanations of bodhisattvas or enlightened beings. Different schools of Buddhism have different important devas, as they are often derived from pre-Buddhist cultures and

religions and not from Buddhist philosophy. Devas are spiritual beings by nature – their form is usually described as bodies or emanations of light or energy. They are, however, often depicted in physical form, and there are many images of devas or dharmapalas, particularly in Tibetan Buddhist iconography.

Devas normally do not interfere in human affairs, but as Buddhist teacher Lama Surya Das notes, they have been known to rejoice, applaud, and rain down flowers for good deeds performed in the world. In Thailand, it is believed that devas approve of people meditating and will harass people of whose behaviour they don't approve. The bodhisattva of compassion, known as Kwan Yin in Chinese and Chenrezig in Tibetan, is widely viewed as a sort of Buddhist angel. The bodhisattva's original Sanskrit name, *Avolokiteshvara*, means 'hearer of the 10,000 cries' – that is, he or she (the bodhisattva is male in the original Buddhist texts, but is represented as female in many Buddhist schools) perceives the suffering of all sentient beings. In some sects, reciting her name is believed to summon her aid.

'Reciting the name' does not mean just saying it. The reciting is an expression of entrusting ourselves to our true nature, or if you will, entrusting ourselves to life. Recitation is of no effect, in terms of immediate help, if it is not done with absolute sincerity.

MORMONS

It is said that Moroni , a mortal man, was the last prophet and author of the last book in the *Book of Mormon*. His life spanned the latter part of the fourth century and the early fifth century. He led ten thousand troops in the last battle against the Lamanites, serving under his father Mormon, who was commander in chief. Prior to the final war, Mormon had abridged the plates of Nephi that covered a thousand years of his people's history. He commanded Moroni to conclude the Nephite record by writing 'the sad tale of the destruction of their people' and to preserve all the sacred writings.

Fourteen hundred years later this same Moroni, now an angel and heavenly messenger 'sent from the presence of God', appeared to Joseph Smith, a 17-year-old youth, on the night of September 21, 1823, and told him of the sacred records deposited in a stone box in a nearby hill in what is now Ontario County, New York, within a few miles of Joseph's home. Moroni appeared to Joseph more than 20 times during the next six years, tutoring him for his calling as a prophet and giving counsel and information concerning the acquisition, translation and guardianship of the *Book of Mormon* plates.

Joseph Smith went on to become the founding prophet of the Church of Jesus Christ of Latter Day Saints (LDS) and Mormonism is a term used to describe the religious and ideological elements of this movement. Golden replicas of the Angel Moroni sit atop many LDS temples, especially the newer ones. So Mormonism as we know it is a relatively recent religion, but it shares many of the same beliefs as Judaism and Christianity.

The Restoration of the Gospel through the Angel Moroni – Mormonism teaches – was prophesied by the Apostle John: 'And I saw another angel fly in the midst of heaven, having the everlasting gospel to preach unto them that dwell on the earth, and to every nation, and kindred, and tongue, and people' (Rev. 14:6).

Mormonism, unlike virtually all other religious philosophies, makes no real distinction between men and angels. According to the Mormon Apostle, Bruce R. McConkie, angels are messengers of God who may be one of five different classes of people (i.e., His offspring):

1. Pre-existent spirits: those people who have yet to come to earth to take on bodies.

2. Translated beings: those people (supposedly like the inhabitants of the city of Enoch in the Book of Genesis who were 'taken') who passed into immortality without experiencing death.

3. Spirits of just men made perfect: these are the spirits of men who have worked out their salvation, but are awaiting the day of the resurrection.

4. Resurrected personages: men like John the Baptist, Moroni, Michael, Gabriel, Raphael, Moses, and Elijah.

5. Righteous mortal men who have yet to die.

Though called by different names, benevolent spirit beings quite similar to angels can also be found within other religions, mythologies and lore. All of these have similar functions as helpful spirit messengers, or angels.

Many people also believe in demons and regard them as fallen angels. This teaching originated in the Hebrew text of Isaiah about Lucifer being cast out of heaven with one third of the angels following him to the earth. When the text was written, Lucifer actually referred to a Babylonian king, but later interpretation of the same text changed Lucifer into Satan, commonly believed by many now to be the 'Devil'.

. . . .

Hush! My dear, lie still and slumber,

Holy angels guard thy bed!

Heavenly blessings without number

Gently falling on thy head

ISAAC WATTS

. . . .

ANGELS
IN
HISTORY

Religion teaches us that angels are supernatural beings that act as mediators between man and God. But what may shock some of us is the idea that angels exist outside of religion with a rich heritage in history and pagan cultures.

It is very difficult to strip the mantle of religion from angels and look at them as something other than theological beings, but objectivity demands that I do so.

The idea of angels is rooted in ancient civilisations such as the Babylonians and Assyrians whose writings include the word *Karabu* or *Kuribu*, winged protective deities, which according to the linguistic scholar Roland De Vaux means 'great, mighty or blessed' depending on interpretations, but is a cognate for cherubim and came to refer in particular to the spirits which served the gods.

The Greeks believed in *Daimones*, personal guiding spirits that attach to individual humans; divine beings that worked between the gods and mankind.

The Roman Genii were believed to be assigned to every person in pairs with one being good and the other evil.

Modern day ideas of guardian angels seem to have incorporated a bit from all three of these ancient types of spirits.

These, however, were not the only influences that shaped angelic beliefs. Primitive tribal cultures also influenced the ideas concerning angels. Tribes commonly hold beliefs in nature spirits and guardian spirits of different sorts, although these spirits often appear in animal form. Like angels, these spirits are typically helpers who watch over tribe members, assisting in spiritual development, while also providing supernatural powers.

Angels also have commonality with spirit guides – benevolent spirits who protect, guide and provide spiritual insight to those on earth. Like angels, they are good spirits, believed to be assigned to a person from birth to death, assisting him or her in their life journey. Like archangels, they may also appear in someone's life for a short period in order to bring special guidance and assistance for particular concerns. These spirits are believed to be the souls of people who once lived on the earth, but have become enlightened with spiritual wisdom. Some think these spirits are entrenched in Native American, Chinese or Egyptian cultures, due to the perceived wisdom found within those cultures, but that is probably a stereotype, rather than a truth. Spirit guides have been found within Gnosticism, spiritualism and other beliefs, as well as being a term used by psychics and mediums to describe spiritual counsellors of persons living in a physical body.

The point is that angels and spirits have been part of almost everyone's ethos and are likely to continue to be so. Whether they are a crutch for us to lean on or a firm belief that our world is populated with something other than tangible flesh and blood, so be it.

> The golden moments in the stream of life rush past us and we see nothing but sand; the angels come to visit us, and we only know them when they are gone.
>
> GEORGE ELIOT

ANGELS
IN ART

Throughout history, painters and sculptors have concentrated on spiritual subjects. The earliest known angel image depicted in Christian art is a fresco that dates back to the second century. It is the Annunciation scene found in the cemetery of St Priscilla. The same subject matter was executed again a century later, also being found in the cemeteries of saints Peter and Marcellinus, all in the vicinity of Rome. These paintings include the *Archangel Gabriel*, depicted in human form, dressed in a tunic and pallium (a circular band about two inches wide, worn about the neck, breast, and shoulders, and having two pendants, one hanging down in front and one behind).

A fourth century painting entitled *The Good Angel* also shows an angel as having a human form. These angels had no wings or halos, perhaps so as not to mimic the pagan deities.

From the reign of Roman Emperor Constantine who made Christianity into a State religion, a new type of angel with wings appears in Christian art.

Classical winged gods, such as Cupid, Hermes and Perseus, as well as the ancient winged gods of Mesopotamia, were likely the inspiration for wings that would eventually be added to angels after the fourth century.

Halos did not float above the heads of the few angels depicted in early Christian art until after the fourth century, either. A halo was a symbol of character, traditionally only painted above pagan gods or Roman Emperors. It is probably for this reason that halos above angels were avoided. When Christian Emperors began having their portraits painted with halos above their heads, halos were soon the rage, finding their way to adorning the head of Jesus, then later the heads of angels by the fifth century in Christian art.

Since then, angels have found their way into countless Christian artworks.

RUSSIAN ICONS
For over 1,000 years Russian Orthodox Christianity inspired and shaped the spiritual

and cultural foundation of Russian society. Icons are the manifestation of this faith and include pictures of Christ, the Virgin Mary, saints and religious historical events. The *ikona*, or Russian icon, derives its name from the Greek word *eikon*, meaning 'image'. After the mixture of Greco-Roman and Syrian art that gave birth to icons was modified in Byzantium, that tradition was passed on to Russia when it was converted to Christianity in 988 AD. The Russians modified it in ways that reflected their own skills and character.

Icons painted in the traditional or 'old' style are executed in a nonrealistic, stylised manner intended to reveal the spiritual nature of the figures depicted rather than accurate anatomical detail. Background hills and buildings are stylised as well. Everything is abstracted from reality to depict a transfigured, timeless world in which material laws of form and substance are transcended.

Russian icon painting had its greatest period of development between the years 1350 and 1650. Between 1860 and 1880 the production of icons reached massive proportions, with entire towns of painters and craftsmen producing them. During the Russian Revolution (1915-1917), the Bolsheviks took power and proclaimed an end to all religious activity, burning icons in public bonfires throughout the country. After the break-up of the Soviet Union in 1991, the few surviving icons slowly emerged back into public view.

ARTISTS WHO HAVE PORTRAYED ANGELS:

Duccio di Boninsegna (1255 – 1318) was an Italian painter from Siena, traditionally identified as the first master of the Sienese school. He painted *Angel Announcing the Death of Our Lord to Mary*.

Giotto di Bondone (1267 – 1337) was an Italian painter and architect from Florence. He is generally considered to be first in a line of great artists who contributed to the Italian Renaissance. He painted *The Angel Gabriel Sent by God*, 1306.

Simone Martini (1284 – 1344) was a major figure in the development of early Italian painting and greatly influenced the development of the International Gothic style. It is thought that he was a pupil of Boninsegna. He painted the *The Angel of the Annunciation*, c.1333.

Fra (Il Beato) Angelico, born Guido di Pietro (1395 – 1455), came from Viccio, Italy and became a Dominican Monk. His art combined the religious style of the Middle Ages with that of the Renaissance. He painted *Madonna and Child with Four Angels*, c.1425.

Masaccio, born Tommaso Cassai (1401 – 1428), came from Tuscany and was the first great painter of the Quattrocento period of the Italian Renaissance. Despite his brief career, he had a profound influence on other artists. He was one of the first to use scientific perspective and he moved away from the Gothic style of his predecessors to a more natural and realistic mode. He painted *The Virgin and Child with Angels*, 1426.

Piero della Francesca (1412 – 1492) was an Italian artist of the early Renaissance. His contemporaries thought of him as a mathematician, but now he is chiefly appreciated for his art. He painted *Palo Montefeltro (The Madonna with Child, Angels, Saints and Federico da Montefeltro)*, 1474.

Leonardo da Vinci (1452 – 1519) was a master of many trades: scientist, mathematician, engineer, inventor, anatomist, painter, sculptor, architect, botanist, musician and writer; the archetypal 'Renaissance Man'. He is considered to be one of the greatest painters of all time and maybe the most diversely talented person to date. He painted *Annunciation*, 1470-1475.

Raphael, born Raffaello Sanzio (1483 – 1520), was an Italian painter and architect of the High Renaissance. Together with Michelangelo and Leonardo, he forms the trinity of great masters of that period. Raphael's most famous painting of angels is the detail from the *Sistine Madonna*.

Michelangelo Buonarroti (1475 – 1564) lived to the venerable old age of 88. He was a painter, sculptor, architect, poet and engineer and despite the fact that his life's work was all contained within the arts, is considered a contender for the same title of 'Renaissance Man' as Leonardo, his rival and fellow Italian. He was the first Western artist to have his biography published in his lifetime. His most famous angel painting is *Angel Holding a Candelabra*, 1495.

Michelangelo Caravaggio (1571 – 1610) was an Italian considered the first great representative of the Baroque school of art. Famous and influential while he lived his mainly dissolute life, he was almost entirely forgotten for centuries after his death until the 20th century when his contributions to art were rediscovered. He painted *St. Matthew and the Angel*, 1602.

Guido Reni (1575 – 1642) was born in Bologna to a family of musicians, Reni's frescoed ceiling of the central hall of Casino dell'Aurora located in the grounds of the Palazzo Pallavicini-Rospigliosi is considered his masterpiece. He painted *Angel of the Annunciation*, year unknown.

Peter Paul Rubens (1577 – 1640) was a prolific 17th century Flemish Baroque painter. His commissioned works were mostly religious subjects and 'history' paintings which included mythological and hunt scenes. Possibly his most famous painting of angels is *Fall of the Rebel Angels*, 1618-1620.

Anthony Van Dyck (1599 – 1641) was a Flemish Baroque artist who became the leading court painter in England. He also painted biblical and mythological subjects, was an accomplished draughtsman and an innovative force in watercolour and etching. He painted *The Madonna and Child With Two Musical Angels*, year unknown.

Rembrandt van Rijn (1606 – 1669) was a Dutch painter and etcher. Considered one of the greatest painters in history, Rembrandt created many brilliant portraits of his contemporaries, self-portraits and scenes from the Bible. One of his better known angel images is *Abraham Entertaining the Angels*, 1656, which was etched copperplate with drypoint.

Bartolomé Esteban Murillo (1617 – 1682) was a Spanish painter and one of the most important figures in the Baroque movement. Although he is best known for his religious works, he also produced a considerable number of appealing paintings of contemporary women and children. His oil painting *Four Angels* was completed *c*.1660.

Giovanni Battista Tiepolo (1696 – 1770) was a Venetian painter and printmaker. As well as Venice, he also worked in Germany and Spain, producing wonderful frescoes. A fine example of Tiepolo's work was a pen and ink drawing *Three Angels Appearing to Abraham*, *c*.1728-1730.

William-Adolphe Bouguereau (1825 – 1905) was a French traditionalist painter who was very popular in his time. He was almost destined to go into the family wine and olive oil business until his uncle, a curate, intervened and taught him classical and biblical subjects. Although he created an idealised world in his painting, which mostly focused on the female form, his almost photo-realistic style brought his goddesses, nymphs, shepherdesses and madonnas to life in a way that was very appealing to his rich patrons. Bouguereau completed many angel paintings including *Angels Playing Violins*.

Gustave Doré (1832 – 1883) was a French artist, engraver, illustrator and sculptor. He was born in Strasbourg and his first illustrated book was published at the age of 15. He was an exceedingly prolific illustrator and his later work included the *Rime of the Ancient Mariner, Paradise Lost* and *The Divine Comedy*.

ANGEL OF THE NORTH
The *Angel of the North* is a contemporary sculpture, designed by Antony Gormley, located in Gateshead, England. As the name suggests, it is a steel sculpture of an angel,

standing 20 metres (66 feet) tall, with wings measuring 54 metres (178 feet) across, making it wider than the Statue of Liberty's height. The wings themselves are not planar, but are angled 3.5 degrees forward, which Gormley has said aims to create 'a sense of embrace'. It stands on a hill on the southern edge of Low Fell overlooking the A1 and A167 roads into Tyneside and the East Coast Main Line rail route.

The sculpture was commissioned in 1995 and erected in February 1998.

All in the wild March morning
I heard the angels call;
It was when the moon was setting,
and the dark was over all;
The trees began to whisper,
and the wind began to roll,
And in the wild March-morning
I heard them call my soul.

THE MAY QUEEN, ALFRED, LORD TENNYSON

ANGELS
IN MUSIC

Angels have long been written about in song, going back to early hymns and holiday carols. The heavenly images have been used to describe those that are adored, cherished and held close to the heart. A recent search on lyrics concerning angels came up with a varied listing of songs, covering all forms of music from classical to rock, theatrical to rap, and country to lullaby. Here is a sampling of some of the songs that I am familiar with.

Angels from the Realms of Glory – James Montgomery
Hark the Herald Angels Sing – Felix Mendelssohn
Waft Her, Angels (Jephtha) – George Frideric Handel
Angel Music – Barberi Paull Feit

The album *Made in Heaven* – recorded in the final months of Freddie Mercury's struggle with AIDS – features an untitled track. It lasts for 22 minutes and is hardly audible, but it sounds eerie and heavenly. It is supposed to chronicle the 22 years between Queen's first and last album, but I always supposed it was about Freddie, because at the end, it sounds like he is leaving this earthly life.

Many artists have recorded songs titled simply *Angel*. Some of the more popular are Madonna, Aerosmith and Jimi Hendrix. One of the earlier pop songs was *Earth Angel* by The Penguins in 1954; even earlier was Matt Dennis' and Earl Brent's *Angel Eyes* which became a hit for Tommy Dorsey's vocalist Frank Sinatra in 1946.

Perhaps the most popular angel song in the last decade or so is *Angels*, written by Robbie Williams and Ray Hefferman. Guy Chambers transformed it into Williams' biggest worldwide selling single when it was released at Christmas 1997. As the song was unknown in the US, Jessica Simpson recorded it in 2004, but in the UK, most of the reviews have been unimpressed with her take on it.

So the fascination with angels in song goes on.

....

Philosophers have argued for
centuries about how many
angels can dance on the head
of a pin, but materialists have
always known it depends on
whether they are
jitterbugging or dancing
cheek to cheek.

TOM ROBBINS

....

ANGELS IN FILMS

Our modern culture is curiously enamoured with angels. This is by no means an exhaustive list of angel films, but it contains some perennial favourites.

Here Comes Mr Jordan (1941)

A clever, charming and ingenious fantasy that was a popular hit in its day. Following an air crash, Joe Pendleton, a boxer, is accidentally taken to heaven 50 years too early by an overzealous angel who wrongly assumes that he is about to die. The angel brings Joe to his supervisor, Mr Jordan, who decides to provide Joe with a new body. The plot is preposterous, but it is all very good fun with a wonderful cast.

It's a Wonderful Life (1946)

An American film produced and directed by Frank Capra, this was loosely based on a short story, *The Greatest Gift*. It takes place in a fictional town shortly after WWII. A man called George Bailey plans to commit suicide on Christmas Eve, and this gains the attention of his guardian angel, Clarence, who is sent to help him. Most of the film is told through flashbacks spanning George's life and narrated by two unseen angels who are preparing Clarence for his mission. This is a classic staple of Christmas television around the world.

Heaven Can Wait (1978)

This was one of the excellent remakes of *Here Comes Mr Jordan* with the Pendleton character now a football player accidentally selected to die after a car accident. He bargains with celestial executive Mr Jordan and gets to live again in someone else's body; that of a millionaire whose wife is plotting to kill him.

Wings of Desire (1987)

This is a fable about two angels visiting present-day Berlin and encountering the past and love. One angel decides he wants to be human because he has fallen for a circus performer, but this proves to be more difficult than it seems.

The Prophecy (1994)

An ancient Bible is found on the body of a

dead angel, which contains a previously unknown chapter of the Bible telling of a second war to be waged by angels on earth. That war is about to occur, led by the archangel Gabriel whose jealousy of God's love for humans has turned him malevolent and bloodthirsty.

Michael (1996)

John Travolta stars as a grubby angel living in the backwoods of Iowa who's got one last good deed to do before heading back to heaven. The winged Michael is hardly the image of a perfect angel. He's scruffy, unshaven, eats sweetened cereal by the box-full and chain-smokes all day long. But when hard-boiled tabloids learn of Michael's alleged existence and head to Iowa to check him out, Michael turns their hearts into slush. There's more to the story, but in essence Michael is about the effect that this enchanting angel has on the earthbound humans around him.

City of Angels (1998)

In this semi-remake of *Wings of Desire*, the heartfelt storyline is of an angel that chooses to fall from his angel status (choosing human life over eternity) in his desire to be with a girl he's in love with.

Dogma (1999)

This film unsurprisingly offended some religious groups when it was released in the US. Two fallen angels discover there is a portal back to heaven; a loophole that will allow them back. The only problem is that it will destroy humanity because it would prove God wrong. A non-believer is called upon to stop them with the help of two guardians and others.

Angels in America (2003)

In this screen version of a play, *Angel*, Emma Thompson must alert an AIDS patient that he is a prophet who can save himself and the rest of the world by stopping humanity's progress. He/she may have the look of an archetypal angel with flowing locks, Grecian robes and wings, but this heavenly hermaphrodite is anything but chaste.

Angels
in
Literature

Many famous authors have written about angels. Some of these stories are allegories, some are serious, some are funny and others are utterly bizarre. Here are some that tickle my fancy.

The Last Trump by Isaac Asimov
In this science fiction short story, it is decided that the Day of Resurrection is due on earth, despite the protestations of Etheriel, a junior Seraph with responsibility for the world. While he seeks an audience with the Chief to plead for a stay of execution for his planet, the Last Trump is sounded, and as of January 1, 1957, time comes to a stop on earth.

Etheriel has his meeting with the Chief and argues that the date is meaningless and therefore the Day of Resurrection is meaningless. The Chief agrees and declares that it will come only when all the peoples of the earth agree on a common date. The world is instantly restored to normality.

The Angel of the Bridge by John Cheever
This almost unknown story is about phobias in the author's family. His mother will not travel by air; his brother is afraid of elevators and the narrator himself develops a fear of bridges which manifests when he is driving a car across one. He attempts to conceal his panic from his wife and children. Taking his daughter back to school in New Jersey one Sunday morning, he almost faints on the George Washington Bridge. He takes a shorter bridge on the way home, but in the middle of it he is forced to stop. A young girl hitchhiker gets into his car. She is carrying a harp and tells him that she is a folk singer. Her appealing quality restores his equilibrium and he successfully crosses the bridge.

The Angel of the Odd by Edgar Allen Poe
This story illustrates the lighter side of Poe in which the narrator reads a story about a man who died after accidentally swallowing a needle. He decides that humanity is too gullible and vows never to be taken in thus. At this point a creature appears and in a thick German accent, announces he is the Angel of the Odd and that he is responsible for causing such strange events. The man

drives the angel away and has a drunken nap, but oversleeps and misses an appointment to renew his fire insurance. Of course his house catches fire and his only way out is to climb out of a window using a ladder the crowd below has provided him with. But as he attempts to do so, a hog brushes against the ladder, so the man falls, breaking his arm.

It appears he is unlucky in love also. He woos a rich woman to be his wife, but this ends badly when she realises he is wearing a wig (he singed his hair off during the fire). Another woman he is interested in also leaves him, believing he has ignored her, when in truth, he has got something in his eye and is momentarily blinded.

He decides to commit suicide by drowning, so he takes off his clothes by the river and then chases after them when a crow runs off with 'the most indispensable portion'. He accidentally runs off a cliff, grabs on to the rope of a hot air balloon just happening to be passing by and the Angel of the Odd reappears, forcing him to admit that bizarre things really can happen. But he can't physically make the pledge the Angel demands because of his broken arm, so the Angel cuts the rope and the man falls down through the chimney into his newly rebuilt house.

A Very Old Man with Enormous Wings by Gabriel Garcia Marquez

In this short story for children, a couple find a very old man in their courtyard during a stormy afternoon. He has enormous wings and struggles to get up from the mud. The couple try to speak to him, but he speaks a different language. A neighbour arrives who tells them that the old man is an angel who has come to take their ill child. The father locks the angel in a chicken coop overnight. The next morning the local priest tests the old man to see if he really is an angel. The entire community comes to see the results, which aren't clear. The mother, who doesn't want everyone in her house, decides to charge a fee to see the angel. With the money collected, the family gets rich and builds a mansion. The crowd has lost interest by now in the angel because another weird character has arrived – a woman who disobeyed her parents when she was young and has been transformed into a tarantula. The townspeople toss meatballs into her mouth so that she can continue to tell her story of misfortune. Meanwhile, the angel, no longer trapped in the chicken coop, leaves and flies away.

Lady Merion's Angel by Jane Yolen
This is a funny, upbeat tale of a young woman's experiences with a small, cherubic angel that wanders into her prized, immaculate garden. Somewhat spoiled and unhappy that she seems no longer the centre of her father's universe, Lady Merion greets the angel first as 'a welcome distraction' and then as an irritant that may mess up her flowers the way her half-brother Clyve had ruined her tapestry. The little angel quietly but determinedly inspires a short journey of self-discovery in Lady Merion, who realises in her heart there is more love and compassion than anger.

TALKING TO ANGELS
Almost 200 years after poet William Blake died and was buried in a pauper's grave in London, thousands of people flocked to exhibits of his work in major museums on both sides of the Atlantic. Although his talent was largely unrecognised in his own lifetime, Blake eventually achieved fame as a poet, a painter and a pioneer engraver, exerting a lasting influence in both literature and graphic arts.

Blake believed much of his inspiration came from his lifetime encounters with angels. Born in London in November 1757, young William was only 10 years old when he saw a vision of angels clustered in the branches of a tree near his home. From then on, wherever he went, Blake saw visions from the other world, from angels in a hayfield, to apparitions of monks in Westminster Abbey. He talked with the angel Gabriel and the Virgin Mary as well as other historical figures.

THE ANGELS
OF MONS

During the Great War thousands came to believe that a miracle happened during the British Army's first desperate clash with the advancing Germans at Mons in Belgium. In some versions a vision of St George and phantom bowmen halted the German troops, while others claimed angels had thrown a protective shield around the British, saving them from disaster.

The battle of Mons took place on 23 August 1914 and within weeks the story of the 'angels of Mons' had become legend. By the end of the war it was thought unpatriotic, even treasonable, to doubt the claims were based on fact.

The Battle of Mons was the first major action by the British Army in World War I. After the forced withdrawal of French and Belgian forces, the British were left exposed and while they fought valiantly, they too were forced to take a costly retreat in the face of overwhelming German forces. In the midst of this retreat a strange apparition of angels holding back the Germans was claimed to occur. It was said that the angels appeared as larger than men, with a central angel in bright light, wings extended, seemingly protecting the two smaller angels in the face of the Germans. The British interpreted this phenomenon as St George, and the story was used in the recruitment of British soldiers.

But did it really happen? The seed for the legend may have been planted by occult novelist Arthur Machen, who wrote a short story in the *London Evening News* about a month after the battle called The Bowmen. To his dying day, Machen insisted the story was fictional and it wasn't specifically about Mons. In fact, it wasn't even about angels. The story relates that a soldier prayed to St George, who brought back a spectral host of bowmen from the Battle of Agincourt who fought on the side of the British. But a number of soldiers present at the battle swore that St George himself had appeared at the battle and staved off the Germans. Something did cause the Germans to waver, for a time they recoiled and withdrew which allowed the British to retreat, but was it St

George? The story of the Angels of Mons bears so little resemblance to Machen's story that it is difficult to imagine that it was the seed that led to the legend.

Sometimes legend becomes fact in its constant repetition. It also depends on who is telling the story, which received a remarkable boost when one of Britain's foremost historians appeared to endorse the idea that there had been heavenly intervention on behalf of the retreating British Expeditionary Force in August 1914.

The British force was in position by 20 August, though far from knowing that the Germans were anywhere near. It fumbled forward, reached the mining town of Mons on 22 August. There the Germans blundered into it, equally surprised. On 23 August, two British divisions were attacked by two German army-corps and held them off. The British rifle fire was so accurate – 'fifteen rounds rapid' per minute—that the Germans thought it came from machine guns. In fact the British had two machine guns for each battalion. The battle of Mons was a small affair by later standards. Still, it was the first British battle and also the only one where supernatural intervention was observed, more or less reliably, on the British side. Indeed the 'angels of Mons' were the only recognition of the war vouchsafed by the Higher Powers.

Abstracted from *The First World War* by AJP Taylor (1963)

Most cite a lack of direct accounts as being supporting evidence that the vision never happened. However, some direct accounts do in fact exist of the Angels of Mons.

In *The Angel of Mons* published in 2005, David Clarke writes, 'The defining moment came with the story of Miss Marrable, the daughter of a clergyman, who claimed she had first hand evidence from two army officers. They had seen "a troop of angels" appear between the British and the German lines at a crucial point in the retreat from

Mons, leading the enemy cavalry to stampede in terror'. Her story was enthusiastically taken up as the proof that would confound the sceptics. When Marrable was eventually traced and questioned it was found that she had been misquoted and had no idea who the officers were, if they even existed. This revelation was ignored by those promoting the claims. In subsequent reprintings of the story, her denial was ignored and her name removed. From this point onwards, the boundary between literary invention and real 'experience' became increasingly blurred.

....

We are each of us angels with only one wing, and we can only fly by embracing one another.

LUCIANO DE CRESCENZO

....

Rallied against Machen in 1915 were the believers in 'divine intervention.' The patriotic author Harold Begbie hastily published *On the Side of the Angels*, subtitled 'an answer to Arthur Machen.' Begbie argued that Machen had exploited a true story for his own commercial ends, or that he had been inspired by a telepathic vision from the brain of a dying soldier at Mons. His book presented the 'eyewitness' accounts of soldiers that he claimed proved Machen was wrong, but his argument was shattered when a key testimony, given under oath by a soldier from the Cheshire regiment, was revealed as a hoax. Begbie also relied upon the dubious evidence of a nurse, Phyllis Campbell, who claimed to have cared for wounded and dying soldiers who had seen the angels. But as Machen pointed out, none of the witnesses could be identified by name: 'Someone (unknown) has met a nurse (unnamed) who has talked to a soldier (anonymous) who has seen angels. But THAT is not evidence'.

Machen used his position as a leader writer

for the *Evening News* to challenge Begbie and Campbell, demanding they produce the names of the soldiers who had made these statements before they could be accepted as evidence. Unable to answer, Campbell claimed there was a Government conspiracy to hide the truth. The soldiers who had seen the angels could not be named, she claimed, because of a cover-up. Those who had witnessed wonders on the battlefield were forbidden by the British Army to discuss what they had seen, but Campbell promised that 'the evidence exists . . . and when the war is over and the embargo of silence is removed, Mr Machen will be overwhelmed with corroborative evidence.'

Did Angels save the British Army in August of 1914, or did a public desperate for good news latch onto a fictional story and mould it into a legend? We can't be certain. But the fact remains that the Germans did waver in the face of something, whether it was fierce British firepower, or angelic intervention on the side of the British Army. If nothing else, the fantasy proved a remarkable morale booster in Britain at a time when military success on the battlefield was much needed.

ANGELS
TODAY

GUARDIAN ANGELS IN NEW YORK
Until I left New York in 1972, I thought nothing of travelling via public transportation. But by 1979, violence and crime were so widespread in New York City that Curtis Silwa, an American anti-crime activist, decided to take the situation in hand and created the 'Magnificent 13', a group dedicated to combating violence and crime on the New York City subways (underground system). At the time, New York was the crime capital of the US and was cutting back its municipal services to reduce its debt.

The 'Magnificent 13' grew and became the 'Guardian Angels', a non-profit, unarmed volunteer organisation, trained originally to make citizens' arrests for violent crime. Some people, including the then Mayor Ed Koch, said they were nothing but vigilantes. In any event, the group, garbed in red berets and white T shirts, became recognisable and popular and spawned chapters in 11 countries and more than 100 cities.

A group of 'Guardian Angels' became active in London in 1989, but by 2007 there were only about 12 volunteers remaining, and their activities were minimal. British law requires any citizen acting in self-defence to use only minimal force and possibly this could have been the reason why our Guardian Angels made less of an impact than their American counterparts.

I feel that there is an angel inside me whom I am constantly shocking.

JEAN COCTEAU

SOVIET COSMONAUTS SEE ANGELS
On 5th January 1986, *Parade Magazine*, a US publication that is delivered to a great number of homes every week with their Sunday newspaper, ran an article entitled 'The Best And Worst Of Everything'. The article was a review of the year 1985. Within that article, under the heading 'Best International News' was the following report:

Six Soviet cosmonauts said they witnessed the most awe-inspiring spectacle ever encountered in space – a band of glowing angels with wings as big as jumbo jets. According to 'Weekly World News', cosmonauts Vladimir Solevev, Oleg Atkov and Leonid Kizim said they first saw the celestial beings last July, during their 155th day aboard the orbiting 'Salyut 7' space station. As the cosmonauts were performing experiments, a brilliant orange cloud enveloped them, blinding them temporarily and when their eyes cleared, they saw the angels. 'What we saw', they said, 'were seven giant figures in the form of humans, but with wings and mist-like halos, as in the classic depiction of angels. Their faces were round with cherubic smiles'. The heavenly visitors, they said, followed them for about 10 minutes and vanished as suddenly as they had appeared.

However, 12 days later, cosmonauts Svetlana Savitskaya, Igor Volk, and Vladimir Dzhanibevok, who had just joined the others on the space station, also saw the beings.

'They were glowing', they reported. 'We were truly overwhelmed. There was a great orange light, and through it, we could see the figures of seven angels. They were smiling as though they shared a glorious secret, but within a few minutes, they were gone, and we never saw them again'.

It is not because angels are holier than men or devils that makes them angels, but because they do not expect holiness from one another, but from God alone.

WILLIAM BLAKE

HOW TO MAKE A SNOW ANGEL

1. Make sure someone is with you (hopefully someone with a camera phone or camera).

2. Bundle yourself up in warm clothing, including a hat and gloves. (Only Kelly D, my eldest granddaughter does it in stiletto heels!)

3. Find a large enough clean patch of snow that hasn't been walked in.

4. Fall gently into the snow on your back.

5. Keeping your body flat, swoop your arms lightly through the snow between your head and your waist.

6. Move your legs as far apart as possible, then together. Pretend you are doing jumping jacks lying down. Repeat arm and leg movements until you have made an impression in the snow.

7. Your friend should stand at your feet and pull on your arms to help you up.

8. Get up without stepping on your snow angel or making a handprint in it.

9. Take a picture of your snow angel and then help your friend to make one.

Real-life
Angel
Encounters

ANGEL ENCOUNTERS

Unless there has been mass hysteria on a global level for thousands of years, angels are real. People have seen them, heard them, smelled them or sensed them, as well as dreamed about them.

While most of the people who have shared their stories with me have been certain that there was angelic intervention in their lives, I have had several experiences in mine that I think are likely to have been angels guarding me.

When I was a tiny baby, it seems that I had some sort of convulsion, started turning blue and stopped breathing. My father, who was rarely around the house in the middle of the day, happened to be there. He really didn't know what to do, but had a cooler head than my mother and from what I heard, he 'received the suggestion' that he ought to breathe into my mouth. Whatever, he 'saved' me and I returned to my normal rosy colour.

Many women sail through pregnancy, but I never had a very easy time, either during or while giving birth. Without giving you the gory details, I could have died giving birth to my first child and miraculously both she and I ended up fine. I was very ill throughout my second pregnancy and when the birth started, it was discovered that my daughter was in a breech position. Caesarian was being seriously thought about, when again, amazingly, she was turned right side up by the obstetrician and I gave birth normally.

Those are 'maybe it was an angel' situations, but throughout my life there have been dozens of instances where I have been walking along the street and stumbled (over a crack in the pavement, a kerb or some such). Just at the point where I should have fallen, either arms have come forward to rescue me or I have regained my balance. In the instances where I have fallen, I have not really hurt myself.

I have also tumbled down flights of stairs, and in one bizarre accident, got my stiletto heel caught in the hem of my dress causing me to plunge backwards into my bathtub. I've also been in the sort of car accidents that people do not usually walk away unscathed from, but I have. These were definitely due to my angel(s) who have been very busy keeping me safe.

The following stories have been told to me by people all over the world and I am grateful to them for sharing their experiences with me.

It is not known precisely where angels dwell – whether in the air, the void, or the planets. It has not been God's pleasure that we should be informed of their abode.

VOLTAIRE

ALISON McC

I am not sure if this counts as angels but I do believe that at certain times people are 'sent' to you.

A couple of examples – shortly after my father died, my mother opened the door to a man from the local parish church – he was organising the delivery of the parish magazine and actually wanted the lady next door. My mother explained the situation and in passing mentioned she was recently widowed. He just happened to have a book on handling grief, which he gave to her. That book helped my mother for some years until she passed it on to a friend who had lost her husband.

Another example is an elderly lady friend of mine who was suffering with ill health and feeling a little depressed. She made her way into our local town to meet up with my mother, but was early, so sat on a bench.

Another older lady struck up a conversation with her and it turned out they had both grown up in the same town (not the one they live in now) and knew the same people though they had never met before. By the time my mother had arrived, my friend felt so much happier just because this lady who she never saw again turned to her for a chat.

I have other more vague examples but usually it just happens that when you are stressed or unhappy, someone does something that makes a complete difference to your outlook.

Pay attention to your dreams – God's angels often speak directly to our hearts when we are asleep.

The Angels' Little Instruction Book, Eileen Elias Freeman, 1994

AMY G

Years ago I went to a spiritualist Church. I had a private reading with the minister who was also a healer. She told me I had a Guardian Angel with me in my car. She said I was a fast driver and asked me if I ever experienced the desire to slow down for no reason at all, and I would come upon some circumstance where I was very happy to be travelling slower. I said 'yes'.

I drove the Interstate to and from work and on second-shift hours. Several times I had slowed down and found that the road ahead was slippery, blocked or a cop was set up for speeders. This happened on any of several routes I could take to work. The minister said it was my mother's unborn child sending me messages. I asked my mother if she ever had a miscarriage and she was dismayed. No one knew she had a miscarriage between my sister and second brother. I am the youngest. The Reverend also said that my now dead Aunt Mary and her best friend were watching out for me.

Be an angel to someone else whenever you can,
as a way of thanking God for the help your
angel has given you.

The Angels' Little Instruction Book, Eileen Elias Freeman, 1994

'ANGEL' SAVES BRITISH MAN

Alex Wargacki, 29, lost consciousness as he and a thousand other people scrambled for the only marked exit from a building in Bangkok, which rapidly became a deathtrap as the flames took hold, claiming at least 61 lives.

Mr Wargacki, one of four Britons injured in the blaze, said the walls and ceilings of the Santika club caught fire with terrifying speed after a firework was set off on a stage as partygoers celebrated New Year.

He said: 'Everyone started running for the door. But the door seemed tiny and people were jammed up against it. If there was another way out, none of us knew about it, and all the windows were barred.

'There were flames from the floor to the ceiling. I could hear windows cracking and breaking in the heat.

'I felt myself going unconscious. I knew something was happening to my lungs. I could not breathe. I blacked out and fell to the floor.

'I woke up and heard this voice saying, "Come on. Come on this way". Then I felt myself being dragged towards an exit. A crowd of people parted in front of me and then I was out in the open air. Had it not been for this voice with the hand of an angel I would not be alive today. The voice sounded as if he was Thai. Maybe he was one of the people at the New Year's party.

'Maybe he was a fireman. But when I get out of hospital I want to thank him for sure.'

Maybe he was really an angel!

Reprinted from Telegraph.co.uk
2 January 2009

ANGEL S

I have had my own encounters with angels as my walk has been so close to the Lord and He has always protected me.

I was very young when I had my son and they almost lost me and him during childbirth. I woke up with a woman's voice speaking to me and her hand stroking my hair. She was talking softly and comforting me. She had an accent to her voice and she was letting me know that everything would be OK and she assured me when I asked that she would be back to see me again. I talked to the nurses afterwards and they told me there was no one that worked there fitting her description nor any patient – especially one with an accent. I will not forget her or the tenderness she shared.

I believe that the Lord has brought angels to me on many occasions. I have almost died five times in my life. Once I was in my car travelling from Michigan to Ohio. My son had taken my car in for an oil change but had forgotten to check the tyres as I had asked him to. On the highway it began to rain and my car started to aquaplane towards a semi (lorry) in the lane next to me. The air current from the semi was enough to send my car in the other direction and the car began spinning in the middle of the highway with cars all around me. I remember feeling a cushion around me in the car. Not a cushion of material but a cushion of love and safety. I felt a gentle tap on one of the corners of my car and then the stronger bump on the tail end. It was raining so hard I couldn't see a thing during all of this. When my car finally came to a stop, I was up against the concrete median in the middle of the busy highway facing the oncoming traffic but safely to the side. When the road was clear I started my car up and did a u-turn and headed to safety off the highway.

I will never forget the help I received that day, nor the love that was with me in that car!

BARBARA G

We all have guardian angels. Mine saved my life years ago when my children were small. A drunk driver tried to pass on my left by driving on the median. It ran out, he hit a kerb and flipped, landed in front of me on his roof, totally blocking the lane crossways. Of course I hit the brakes as hard as possible, actually standing on the brake, my head pressing into the headliner so hard it left a permanent dent. All the time I was praying to God to save my life. I had two small children to raise alone. Their father had died the year before.

The drunk's car should have started slowing down when he landed, but the spooky part was, his car was sliding (sending up showers of sparks from the friction as the metal slid across the concrete) exactly as fast as my car was going, just like my guardian angel had put his hand between us. At first I couldn't get over to the next lane on my right because of the traffic, but thank God for smart drivers. The two lanes to my right saw what was happening and pulled over or pulled back. Several cars started honking at me to let me know it was safe to pull over. I did, and as soon as I did, the drunk driver's car slowed immediately and then started rolling and stopped. My perception was all in slow motion; the entire incident is burned into my memory. I know without a doubt that God and my guardian angel saved me. The policeman that took my statement couldn't believe it either, just kept shaking his head saying, 'Man, oh man'.

Millions of spiritual creatures walk the earth unseen,
both when we wake and when we sleep.

John Milton, *Paradise Lost*

CHANTEL C

Once – many years ago, I was driving from Cricklade going through the Leigh when I was convinced I could hear my grandmother telling me to brake. I did brake and at that point a toddler came running from a side gate onto the road. If I hadn't braked, I would have hit the child. The mother came rushing from the garden – someone had visited and left the gate open.

Around the throne of God a band
of glorious angels always stand;
bright things they see, sweet harps
they hold,
and on their heads are crowns of gold.

Some wait around him, ready still
to sing his praise and do his will;
and some, when he commands them, go
to guard his servants here below.

Lord, give thy angels every day
command to guide us on our way,
and bid them every evening keep
their watch around us while we sleep.

So shall no wicked thing draw near,
to do us harm or cause us fear;
and we shall dwell, when life is past,
with angels round thy throne at last.

John Mason Neale

DEE V

When my mother passed away I was not able to attend her funeral and since I could not be there, I set up my living room and had my own memorial for her at the same time as the funeral.

About two weeks later I was ill in bed and NO ONE was home with me as my husband had gone to work and the dog was in the other part of the house. I was in a deep sleep and was suddenly awakened by a kiss on the cheek. I got out of bed and went to see why my husband had come back home, but he was not there nor was anyone else.

I was so shocked by what had happened, I called my husband to see where he was and why he came home and kissed me. He told me he had not been home and that it must have been my mother who came down from heaven and gave me that kiss on my cheek. It was so real that it gave me goose bumps and a warm feeling rushed all over me. Knowing that my mother gave me a kiss was the best medicine I ever needed. I was able to go back to sleep and dream of her in heaven with all the other angels. My health took a turn for the better and I got over my illness and was able to go back to work a few days later.

I thank the Good Lord daily for sending my mother to me when I needed her most.

The guardian angels of life fly so high
as to be beyond our sight, but they are always
looking down upon us.

Jean Paul Richter

DONNA IN MONTICELLO MN

If you are talking about 'seeing' angels then I cannot help. However, I have almost daily encounters from my guides; sometimes my mother and more often, my Dad.

If I ever misplace something, my mother ALWAYS finds it for me and places it where I can see it, or she will keep after me with the location of the item. Last week I left my sunglasses at the gym. It never occurred to me they would be there but my mother kept after me in my thoughts to call the gym and find out. Yep, they were there.

Dad always helps me in the garage if I'm looking for a particular item that is rarely, if ever, used. I just say, 'Dad, I'm sure you know where it is so tell me, okay?' Within seconds he will suggest I look in a particular place and again, that's where it is.

I constantly get guidance in many, many ways throughout the day from my guide(s) and angel(s). The trick is to have an open mind that there may be a suggestion other than what your mind is thinking. Because I am so used to listening to my guides it's hard, right now, to think of an instance. I do realise immediately I was 'helped' and I always, always say thank you. I believe giving thanks opens the portals of communication even more. Maybe it's the positive energy: I really

An angel can illuminate the thought
and mind of man by strengthening
the power of vision.

Saint Thomas Aquinas

ERVENE B

I have had many personal encounters with angels. Here are a few.

I actually believe I've seen the angel of death … or what I think is the angel of death. It was incredibly beautiful … and difficult to explain.

My first dying patient was my daughter's girlfriend's mother, who eventually succumbed to cancer. I worked with her for 18 months before she died, giving her massages and Reiki rather regularly. She was very frail and this helped her pain. Once when I was visiting her in hospital, I saw what I could only describe as a 'living light' beside her bed. It was an incredibly beautiful, feeling light from another dimension; a geometrical light, moving with a radiating 'feeling'. I realised that no one else in the room could see it or feel it. In 'the dimension' where the light was, I couldn't see anything but 'it'. It was not transparent and was like nothing I had ever seen before.

When I was working at an interior design job, one of my co-workers asked me to do healing on a friend of hers who was very ill with jaundice. This patient told me she could see an angel behind me. I assumed it was her angel and told her so. I didn't see it, but the next day her jaundice disappeared and she got better. The result of my 'healing' or intervention from her angel?

Another story. I have a friend who lives in Delaware. At the time we were both struggling with our marriages and bonded. Both of us divorced eventually and remarried. We each have a son and a daughter who used to play together as children. Her son had leukaemia and was in hospital. She phoned me one day and talked to me (it's not uncommon for people to tell me things they don't tell anyone else – it is just the way my ministry works). She could see two angels in her son's room. She described them as being huge. She said the bed was covered in light. Later on, she called me to say there was only one angel. (The boy was in remission and went home. At this point he didn't need two angels.) My friend even saw the angel at her home, kneeling at her son's bed, crying. Angels cry tears of joy! The boy lived another two years.

One of my Reiki masters, a retired school-teacher, also sees angels. She doesn't tell many people about them because she's afraid her children will think she's crazy and not allow her to look after her grandchildren. She says they can be seen up and down the roads. Another friend told me the very same thing and these two women do not even know each other.

I love angels! Both the earthly kind and the ones in spirit. I know a lot of people who see them, or feel them, or smell them. They have a lovely fragrance. I have experienced it myself. One story in particular comes to mind of an angel here on earth.

I had a hospice patient; a beautiful young man with a lovely red-haired wife and two small children. He had Amyotrophic Lateral Sclerosis (ALS), often referred to as 'Lou Gehrig's Disease' in the US. It is a progressive neurodegenerative disease that affects nerve cells in the brain and the spinal cord. He could not move or talk, although he could still blink. His mind was intact, however, and if his wife put a small flashlight on his head and an alphabet board in front of him, he could move his head just enough to spell out words. It was quite a labour talking to him and waiting for him to spell out his responses, but it made him happy.

FAY F

Many bereaved people see white feathers at significant moments and/or places.

TV presenter Gloria Hunniford told Fern Britton and Philip Schofield on *This Morning* that she regularly finds lone feathers, which she believes to be 'messages' from her late daughter.

She said: 'Caron believed feathers were calling cards from angels. It is extraordinary because I am constantly finding isolated feathers, including one in the studio today – even though there were no feathers around. One feather fell at my feet the day of Caron's funeral ... I find it a great comfort.'

For me, it's shooting stars – typical of my angel!!

I do often glance up at the night sky just when a shooting star zips by and always like to imagine Si (my late husband) who spent so many evenings stargazing, sending a little hello.

We cannot but believe that all miracles,
whether wrought by angels or some other
means, are wrought by those who
love us in a true and godly sort.

Saint Augustine

FREDDIE J

I think this guy must have been an angel although he was dressed in a business suit and tie. I was 3½ and my father had very recently died. I started to wet the bed again, so my aunt and my mother put me in the bedroom right next to the bathroom to help me make it on time.

I was very conscientious about this project. One night I woke up in the middle of the night, determined to make it to the bathroom. Now, our bedrooms and bathroom were on the second floor. I got up and there was a man standing right by the window beside my bed. He resembled my father but was not him, although I knew he was there because of my father. I told him I had to go to the bathroom and that I would be right back. He caught the hem of my nightie and said, 'Don't go, Frederica'. I told him that I had to and repeated that I'd be right back; then I jerked my nightie out of his hand.

I rushed into the bathroom without closing the door as I was very anxious to get back to him. When I hurried out, I bumped my head on the corner of the door. When I went back to my bedroom, he was gone and I never saw him again.

The next morning, my mother looked at me with worry in her eyes because I had a bruise on my forehead and a dent. I told her about the man but she didn't pay attention, just hustled me out to the car and took me to the doctor. It turned out that I had a concussion. I told the doctor about my visitor but he just looked at my mother and mentioned that I had a blow to my head and she nodded knowingly.

I was very young, but I KNEW what I saw and it didn't have anything to do with the bump on my head.

Lord, keep your arm around my shoulder and your hand over my mouth. Amen.

JANE L

Twenty-eight years ago this city-bred girl (me) moved from the large city of Milwaukee, Wisconsin, to the desolate woods in the north of the state. I moved there in mid-September but didn't start my job at a hospital 20 miles away until October.

I had to travel dark, curvy, wood-lined roads to the closest town. That year we had an unprecedented early, heavy snowfall. I don't know if I was going to work for the night shift or in the early morning, but I remember it was pitch-dark. The snow was so deep that the bottom of my car dragged in it. The winding roads were unfamiliar to me, there were no tracks to follow and since it hadn't been ploughed yet, there were no snow banks to mark the edge of the road. I was terrified of going off the road and prayed 'let there be a light'. I no sooner said that when I rounded a bend and there was a country church with a lone street light marking the side road. Also there were some tyre tracks from that point on, so at least I knew how to stay on the road. I always remember that incident as a time when my prayers were immediately answered ... by God? Angelic intervention?

For several years one of my nurse co-workers would tell me of her many encounters ... usually with child-like figures. One time during a storm with a power cut, her two children were 'camping out' on the living room floor in sleeping bags so as not to be afraid. My friend 'saw' another blonde girl sitting on the sofa, but her daughter was asleep on the floor. Another time she encountered a boy-child spirit while on a camping trip. This friend accompanied me to visit the daughter of a friend of mine who was known to be psychic. In visiting with us she said she could 'see' my guardian angel and that it appeared to be male. She herself had been sitting at a computer keyboard and she was caused by her own guardian angel to type that his name was Job (as from the Bible). She also felt that the guardian angels one has changed from time to time.

JOHN F

My father had a guardian angel.

My mother rang to inform me that my father was terribly ill in a coma in hospital in England, and that I had to come immediately. At the time I was living in Florida. I got on a plane as fast as I could; one of her neighbours met me at Heathrow and drove me to their flat. Just as I walked through the door, the telephone rang. I picked it up because my mother was in another room. It was one of the nurses at the hospital informing me that my father had just died. He must have known that he could let go because I was there to take care of my mother.

Another much earlier time, when I was a small child, my father was in hospital with a serious, possibly fatal illness. One day he saw a very bright light and saw himself floating, looking down on his body in the bed. Apparently it wasn't his time yet, because something pulled him back and he recovered.

Black as the devil,
Hot as hell,
Pure as an angel
Sweet as love

Charles Maurice de Talleyrand-Périgord, recipe for coffee

JEFF G

Angels don't always come to us in human form. This is a story about a man and a bald eagle in Washington State that circulated around the internet in the last few months. I abstracted this from an email an American friend sent in February.

Freedom and I have been together 10 years. She came into the Sarvey Wildlife Centre as a baby in 1998 with two broken wings. Her left wing doesn't open all the way even after surgery. When Freedom came in, she could not stand. She was emaciated and covered in lice. We made the decision to give her a chance at life, so I took her to the vet's office. We had her in a huge dog carrier with the top off, loaded up with shredded newspaper for her to lie in. I used to sit and talk to her, urging her to live, to fight and she would lay there looking at me with those big brown eyes. We also had to tube feed her. This went on for 4–6 weeks and she still couldn't stand.

It got to the point where the decision was made to euthanise her if she couldn't stand in another week. You know you don't want to cross that line between torture and rehab and it looked like death was winning. She was going to be put down that Friday, and I was supposed to come in on Thursday afternoon. I didn't want to go to the centre that Thursday, because I couldn't bear the thought of her being euthanised; but I went anyway, and when I walked in everyone was grinning from ear to ear. I went immediately back to her cage and there she was, standing on her own, a big beautiful eagle. She was ready to live.

We knew she could never fly, so the director asked me to glove train her. I got her used to the glove, and then to jesses (tethers used to train falcons), and we started doing education programmes for schools in western Washington. We wound up in the newspapers, radio and some TV.

In the spring of 2000, I was diagnosed with Non-Hodgkins Lymphoma. I had stage 3, which is not good (one major organ plus everywhere), so I wound up doing eight months of chemo. When I felt good enough, I would go to Sarvey and take Freedom out for walks. Freedom would also come to me in my dreams and help me fight the cancer.

This happened time and time again. In November 2000, the day after Thanksgiving, I went in for my last check-up. I was told that if the cancer was not all gone after eight rounds of chemo, my last option was a stem cell transplant. Anyway, they did the tests and all the cancer was gone. So the first thing I did was get up to Sarvey and take the big girl out for a walk. It was misty and cold. I went to her flight and jessed her up and we went out front to the top of the hill. I hadn't said a word to Freedom, but somehow she knew.

She looked at me and wrapped both her wings around me to where I could feel them pressing in on my back (I was engulfed in eagle wings) and she touched my nose with her beak and stared into my eyes and we just stood there like that for I don't know how long. That was a magic moment.

We have been soulmates ever since she came into the centre. This is a very special bird.

On a side note: people who were ill would come up to us when we were out and Freedom has some kind of hold on them. Once a guy who was terminal came up to us and I let him hold her. His knees just about buckled and he swore he could feel her power course through his body. I have so many stories like that. I never forget the honour I have of being so close to such a magnificent spirit as Freedom's.

Angels are never too distant to hear you.
Author unknown

KAY H

My mother is my Guardian Angel. Shortly after she passed away, I was driving down a busy street in Des Moines, Iowa (I lived in Des Moines at the time) and I had looked off to the right as I was coming to a junction. All of a sudden I felt this hand on my shoulder and as I looked in front of me, I slammed on my brakes. The car in front of me had slowed down to almost a stop for no apparent reason. The light was green for us, so I do not know why this car slowed down like it did. But I just know that it was my mother looking out for me and it was my mother's hand that was on my shoulder. (As the hand touched my shoulder, I saw an image of my mother.) Had she not put her hand on my shoulder, I would have been in an accident. March 2009 she will have been gone for 25 years and I know that she is ALWAYS with me.

Dogs have angels also, I think.

Do not forget to entertain strangers,
for by so doing some people have
entertained angels without knowing it.
Hebrews 13:2

Just this side of heaven is a place called Rainbow Bridge. When an animal that has been especially close to someone on earth dies, that pet goes to Rainbow Bridge. There are meadows and hills for all of our special friends so they can run and play together. There is plenty of food, water and sunshine and our friends are warm and comfortable. All the animals who were ill and old are restored to health and vigour. Those who were hurt and maimed are made whole and strong again just as we remember them in our dreams of days and times gone by. The animals are happy and content except for one small thing: they miss someone very special to them who had to be left behind. They all run and play together, but the day comes when one suddenly stops and looks into the distance. His bright eyes are intent. His eager body quivers. Suddenly he begins to run from the group, flying over the green grass, his legs carrying him faster and faster. You have been spotted and when you and your special friend finally meet again, you cling together in joyous reunion, never to be parted again. The happy kisses rain upon your face; your hands again caress the beloved head and you look once more into the trusting eyes of your pet, so long gone from your life, but never absent from your heart. Then you cross Rainbow Bridge together.

Author unknown

A man does not always choose what
his guardian angel intends.
Saint Thomas Aquinas

MARGIE L

I don't know if I have a guardian angel *per se*, but I know that an awful lot of things seem to happen in my life that are good with no apparent explanation!

I should start by saying that I believe in angels. I did before the events listed below but now I'm sure.

This happened to my mother a long time ago. She was horribly ill, but had to pick up my father from out of town. She managed to drive to the car park, but passed out. Eventually, my father knocked on the window of the car and roused her. She asked him, 'How did you know I was here?' He said some guy he had never seen before came up to him while he was eating and told him she was in the car park. Considering he had been working that job for six months, it seemed quite unlikely there would have been anyone he hadn't seen before who was dressed as one of the workers. We concluded it was an angel.

In another instance, my mother and I were at Busch Gardens in Tampa at least 15 years ago. We went as part of her birthday week festivities. We wanted badly to go on the open truck tour through the 'Serengeti Plain'. We had missed the morning one so we walked around the park. And around. And around. We were both exhausted. My mother was leaning on her stick. I could hardly take a step my feet were in such excruciating pain. The problem was that we couldn't find the ticket office so we were losing hope. We walked down a path where 'maybe' the office was and could clearly see that there was nothing there. We were both at the end of our tether. My mother leaned against a fence post.

I saw a family a little further down the road, leaning on the fence, looking at the animals. I said to my mother, 'Maybe THEY know where the ticket office is'. I walked (slowly) up to them. It was a man, a woman and two children. I asked and the man said, 'Oh yes!' He knew where it was. I must have passed it;

it was just up the hill and to the right. I cross-examined him pretty crossly. 'Are you sure? We were just up there. There is no ticket office'. 'Yes', he insisted and told me he had been there that morning and bought tickets. 'It's just a tent', he said. 'It doesn't look like a ticket office'. He said he had spoken with a woman and gave me her name. He said it was a great ride, but to hurry because the next one was just about to start. So I did.

I went up the hill, found the place. It was, as he said, just a small tent, not an office so I had walked by it several times. I was so relieved I began to gush that I had been told to come there by a nice family that had taken the morning ride who told me to ask for her because she had been so nice. At that point, I said her name. She said it wasn't her name. I said that it had been in the morning so maybe they had spoken with someone else. She said no, she had been the only one there all day, and no family (or man matching my description) had bought tickets. There had

only been four people on the morning run and it certainly was not any of the people I had seen. I told her that was impossible. He had described the tent and the woman and the ride. She said that might be, but he had not purchased any tickets from her.

I went back down the hill with the tickets to get my mother, still propped up on the fence post. I was so excited to have them that I babbled out the story. We couldn't figure it out. I looked, but the family was gone so I couldn't ask them about it. Then I asked my mother, 'Did they come up here past you?' She said they had not. But they had been where the road ended. There was no other way out except back up the road past my mother. These were our angels. A nice middle class family on a day out at the park. They appeared to relieve our distress. They disappeared when the need was answered.

PAM G

My girlfriends and I were young and dumb … years ago … out drinking and partying like only girls can do. We always thought we had a guardian angel named Ralph De Briccasart. He looked just like Richard Chamberlain in *The Thorn Birds*. We still believe that Ralph took care of us when we were doing these things, good and bad. We called on him a lot. A whole lot. It still works for us 30 years later. We no longer party and get wild like we used to. But he is real to us. There has to be someone there because we never got into anything we could not get ourselves out of. We never got picked up while drinking and we should have had three days in the electric chair at times. We still call on Ralph to pay attention because we may need him. And it works. We love Ralph.

Pam, Susie, Donna, Sonnie and Kitty

If you woo the company of the angels
in your waking hours,
they will be sure to come
to you in your sleep.
G D Prentice

RENEE F

I think there's a lot of sappy stuff going on about and around angels but it hasn't stopped me from having my own affection for and 'belief' in them.

In 1980, after my surgery for diverticulitis during which I almost died, I was walking on the beach in the midst of an absolutely insane panic attack because I was experiencing a lot of pain and was terrified of having to go into the hospital again. Suddenly, I felt my whole body being lifted up and enfolded in a powerful, yet feathery down softness.
A supreme peacefulness and calm flooded my entire being. I felt as if I was floating out of Time and Space as all pain, anxiety, fear and panic fell away.

I don't know how long it lasted in real time; a second or an hour, but that panic never returned! In retrospect, I have always thought of that 'powerful softness' as angel wings wrapped around me attached to some lovely guardian angel to whom I am forever grateful. It was not a visual experience, but it was most certainly a very tangibly physical, visceral, emotional and spiritual one! The memory of it still warms my heart.

Angels are messengers, but sometimes
we misunderstand their language.

Linda Solegato

SALLY L

Sadly, in 1977 our infant daughter died. My husband said that night he dreamed an angel came down and took her soul to heaven and he felt a weight lift from him, knowing she was safe.

> Music is well said to be the speech of angels.
>
> Thomas Carlyle

STUTI D

It was my birthday on November 26th 2008 and as we always do as a family tradition, we were supposed to have dinner at the Golden Dragon Chinese restaurant at the Taj Mahal Hotel in Mumbai that night. However, we decided to cancel our plans and go to the President Hotel and have Italian food instead, since my sister wasn't feeling too well and wanted something light and non-spicy to eat. So we go for dinner to the Trattoria Restaurant instead, and after we were done (around 10 pm), as we were exiting the lobby and waiting for the valet to bring our car, we saw some people running frantically and in panic and found out about the blasts and shooting at the Taj and the Oberoi hotels.

We rushed to our car and drove home immediately. Had we gone to the Golden Dragon that night, we really wouldn't know our fate! It was my sister's health (or angelic intervention) that made us change our mind. While watching the TV coverage after the siege was over, we could identify the very table near the window at the Golden Dragon that we always sat at. It still sends shivers down our spines when we think of that day.

SUSAN H

Yes, I encountered an angel. I was in nursing school, at Valparaiso University in Valparaiso, Indiana. It was December 1986, and I was going into a religion class. I wasn't sure where the classroom was – it had been changed for this class period. I was running late (no surprise there), and it had just begun to snow. I was feeling grumpy, Christmas shopping not done, single parent of a young child and not enough money, too much to do, not enough time, etc.

As I was hustling into the building, there was a man in a wool topcoat, with a hat – much like I would picture Clarence from *It's a Wonderful Life*, with a cardboard box in his hands. He was handing out small bibles from that box. Some were green and some were white. The building was actually a School of Engineering building, not the nursing school. As he saw me approach, he reached into the box and pulled out a white bible. 'For a nurse, a white bible!' he said. At the time, it never occurred to me he should know I'm a nurse! No telltale nursing cap or uniform. So I took the bible, heard his wishes for a Merry Christmas, and hurried into class.

I apologised for being late, and mentioned my brief meeting with the gentleman with the bibles. My classmates said 'what man with bibles?' As I was only about five minutes late, I said 'you had to see him – he was out there in front!'. Several classmates looked out the window, and the gentleman was gone! I ran out to the door, just like in the movies, looking for his footprints and lo! My prints were the only ones out there! That is one encounter I will never forget and it brings tears to my eyes to remember it this long afterwards.

Angels can fly directly into the heart of the matter.

Author unknown

SUSIE B

Well I'm not sure I totally understand what an Angel experience is, but this certainly changed me from a non-believer to a believer in something! It happened in Florida in September this year.

A very good friend named Carole lived there. I'd known her since 1990. She moved to Dubai in 1994 so when I moved there in 1999 she was there for me.

She later moved to Florida and in early 2008 Carole fell ill with cancer.

Another friend, Sue and I wanted to go out to see her all year but for one reason or another Carole kept putting us off (too ill or about to have treatment or she was coming to England, etc).

Eventually we booked to fly out on the 24th September. When we were all packed and ready to go Carole sadly passed away. So the trip was not as we had planned, but we were at least there to help with the funeral and 'see her off'. It was obviously very disappointing and sad for us to have 'missed her'.

We got to see her in the chapel of rest for a final goodbye and then after the funeral service her ashes were scattered out at sea. A small boat took just seven out for this simple service. I didn't go on it, but my friend Sue did. As her eight-year-old son Laurence let the small boat off the side and said goodbye, an amazing sunset lit the sky. It was incredible – the sky was totally covered in GOLD. This may not seem important to most, but all through Carole's life we had said she 'walked on paves of gold' so this was extremely reassuring that it was a sign from her to say all was ok. I actually got a huge amount of comfort from this and felt a huge relief. That was the first sign we thought that all was well with her.

The next evening Sue and I and three other English friends of Carole's went out for dinner to her favourite restaurant. As we drew up to the most amazing hotel I have ever been to, Sue (who sat in front of me in the middle row of a seven seater Lexus) turned sharply to me and said 'oi!' I didn't know what she meant but it turned out she had felt a sharp flick to her ear and thought it was me playing around (the sort of thing Carole always used to do – she was often playing jokes on people or teasing in some way). I hadn't done anything so indignantly said 'what? – I didn't do anything.' At the same time Amalia, who sat next to Sue, said 'oh! what was that? It flew into the front'. She had seen something big and black fly past her.

What happened was that Sue had felt a sharp flick to her ear (which she thought was me) and her black earring flew out of her ear. (Amalia had seen it.) I got out of the car leaving them and the valet parkers to look for it (personally I was thinking 'It's an earring for god's sake! We can find it later! Look at this amazing hotel!').

So I went into the hotel with my mouth open in amazement – it was BEAUTIFUL.

When Sue caught up with me and the others, she was white and said she had goose pimples. The earring had been found in the footwell of the car.

Sue was pleased, but as she walked in she thought 'well I can't wear it because I don't have the butterfly back.' Then as she was about to put it away safely she noticed the back was actually on the earring! We all asked if she had put it in like that, but it was not possible. The back of the earring was too short – it was impossible!

Carole was such a practical joker – she totally believed in the afterlife. If I hadn't been there I would have thought someone was exaggerating, but Sue is not the type to make anything up and we all witnessed it.

SYLVIA B

ANGELA'S LAST VISIT

This may or may not be related to 'Angels' but it is strange that 'Angel' is almost her name!

I was sick with a dose of 'Dubai flu' and sleeping in the spare bedroom. When my husband came to check up on me the next morning, he found me in tears and very upset. I told him that during the night, I had seen or dreamed of my oldest and best friend Angela, who was suffering from pancreatic cancer in the UK and I was convinced that she had passed away or was close to doing so.

My dream, if such it was, went as follows:

I was in her farmhouse to see her and was sitting in her little snug room; no one else seemed to be there. She was upstairs and I called out to let her know that I knew she was ill and didn't want to see anyone, but I had come to see her and it didn't matter that she was not looking at her best – I just wanted to see her. I was sitting in a leather armchair with my back to the half open door and suddenly became aware of her in the hallway outside the room. I was conscious of her 'drifting' past the door and into the kitchen. I stood up and followed her, sensing that this was what she wanted me to do. I walked towards the kitchen door which was ajar and clearly saw the kitchen beyond. I was very familiar with her house and knew that this was her kitchen, being very conscious of the door which was painted black. I pushed the door to open it, but it would not move. I used all my strength, but it was no use, I could not open the door.

It was as if she was teasing me, letting me know that she had come down, but that I was not going to see her again – and in fact, I did not see her again!

Some three hours later, her daughter called me to say her mother had died whilst sitting watching the Cenotaph Memorial Service on Remembrance Day, which was about when I 'saw' her! All very strange, but quite true!

SYLVIA K

I've encountered angels a couple of times. I will share the incident that impacted me most. I'm a person of faith, have a relationship with my Lord Jesus Christ and believe there are angels all around us, watching, caring for us.

In 2000 I became very ill, and after much medical consultation it was deemed that a pacemaker would fix my problem. The morning of the surgery I prayed for competence for the doctors, peace for me and expertise for the nurses looking after me.

Due to other medical issues I could not have a general anaesthetic. The area where the pacemaker was inserted would be frozen and I would be awake; no relaxant was administered.

As I was wheeled into the operating room, this peace flowed over my body like I had never experienced before. And as I lay there waiting for the procedure to begin, I saw four angels surround my bed in the operating room, one at each corner. They were clothed in white gowns, their faces hidden from me. As I said, I was awake for the whole surgery and they were there till the procedure was completed. As the nurse came to wheel me to the recovery room the angels disappeared.

Where the bright seraphim in burning row
Their loud uplifted angel trumpets blow

John Milton, *At a Solemn Musick*

TAMARA A-N

Angels are no strangers in my life ... both my parents are quite spiritual people, a kind of cross between good old fashioned Catholicism and the New Esotericism. My mother started off as a Comparative Religions teacher and progressed on to The Kabbalah. She was also made a Priest of the Liberal Catholic Church many years back. She is also an expert in the Ancient Traditions and Spiritual beliefs of Ancient Cultures and writes books on Esoteric Philosophy. I have been brought up really with a certain amount of belief in Angels as beings who are perhaps a little more 'advanced' cosmically speaking. As a little girl my prayer before bed was based on an old Kabbalistic prayer: 'Great Raphael before me, Gabriel behind me, Uriel to my left and Michael to my right; Around me is the love of the mighty archangels and above my head is the everlasting glory of God'.

However, belief in something is a little different from actually coming across one face to face and having a real time experience of them. It wasn't, looking back, an amazing event of a burning bush that spoke to me, nor was it a huge man with wings .... in actual fact it almost felt normal at the time!

I must have been about 12 or 13. Every year at Easter time and during the Summer holidays, we would all as a family (including grandparents) pile into two cars and drive, like bats out of Hell, down through France to Spain, where we had a little villa in a then unknown and rather unspoilt town called Denia on the Costa Brava. Now it is all urban sprawl and has, unfortunately, become another Benidorm. We absolutely loved these times, because we would visit strange and out of the way historical places and came to know the real old France and old Spain.

This particular year, along with the English grandparents, we took along my Polish grandmother, recently widowed and a devout Catholic. She expressed an interest in seeing some places of Catholic interest, such as Lourdes, The Black Madonna at Montserrat and the Shrine of Saint Theresa of Avila. We did all of these and she dutifully prayed us safely across two countries and several mountain ranges.

My brother and I were pretty 'churched' out by this time and were desperate to get to the sea and the swimming pool!!! So it was with heavy hearts that we got the news that my parents had decided to take a little detour up around the back of Madrid to see one last epic church.

This Church was no ordinary church, but a grand cathedral built after the Spanish Civil War as a memorial to those who had died. It was high up in the mountains, and literally hewn into the rock! To say that it was impressive doesn't do it enough justice. It is massive and awesome. Huge statues of Angels with swords guard the entrance and once through that initial entrance you walk into the cathedral itself which is part of the mountain. We had somehow contrived to get there on a Good Friday ... and a huge mass was being said inside. Twelve priests were saying the mass and the place was filled with people, clergy and incense. My gran was in seventh heaven ... my brother and I were bored out of our brains!!! But we did our bit and sat still and listened to all the nice singing and the droning of the priests and dreamed of the swimming pool.

There was a part of the mass, which I believe was supposed to denote the actual moment of Christ's death on the Cross and all the candles, bar one, were extinguished on the high altar. It must have been at that moment that I opened my eyes, because everything had gone all quiet and deathly still.

I could see the smoke from the candles drifting up from the altar, and as it drifted, it formed itself into a huge shape, like a flying man with wings ... it literally hovered above

TAMARA A-N *(continued)*

the altar and became shimmery and reflected many different lights. For a moment I looked at it not sure what I was seeing, then my heart literally started pounding and I became quite scared, because it really appeared to be an angel looking down on all of us. I was sitting next to my mother and I remember shaking her arm and whispering to her did she see what I was seeing? She looked at me and I could tell that she had seen it too because she'd gone quite white. The shape appeared there, quite still for a few minutes, in fact it was almost as if time stood still ... then slowly it just became smoke again and evaporated into the air.

No one else in my family had seen the 'Angel', even though they were sitting in the same place and had the same vista. It was an extraordinary experience that I shared with my mother. The panicky feeling I now put down to the kind of ice cold awe that people often say they experience at such times, or if they witness something spiritual or extraordinary.

When I write about it now, it doesn't do the experience any justice, it almost seems kind of tame. No, it wasn't a great white light that visited me and spoke to me, but it did have a presence, and the fact that only my mother and I appeared to witness it speaks volumes. I often think about it even now and wonder about it ... it sort of gives me a sense of peacefulness and hope that as little human beings running around a very imperfect world, that there is something greater than ourselves out there. Maybe after all, that's exactly what angels are meant to do?

The magnitude of life is overwhelming.
Angels are here to help us take it peace by peace.
Levende Waters

ROBERT S

The evening of December 21, 1988, Pan Am flight 103 was blown up at 31,000 feet 38 minutes into its journey. The aeroplane exploded and pieces of the plane fell onto the Scottish town of Lockerbie. I should have been on that flight. I was in Newcastle for business meetings and was able to finish my meetings one day earlier than planned. I changed my return flight from London or I would indeed have been on that specific flight.

I recall the next day being in my office in the US and one of my colleagues came to inform me of the disaster – 270 people died; 259 in the plane and 11 on the ground. I became very emotionally upset. I had to leave the office to join my family at home and count my blessings.

Make yourself familiar with angels
and behold them frequently in spirit;
for without being seen,
they are present with you.

Saint Francis de Sales

VIVIAN F

Still reeling from the shock at having been diagnosed with cervical cancer, I was whisked into hospital before I had any further time to consider the implications. I was booked to go under the surgeon's knife at 9:00 a.m. – the first operation of the day. My family, needless to say very anxious to know how the procedure went, waited at home. Little did they know that it would be a long wait!

Each time my husband phoned to see if I was out of surgery, he was told there was a complication and that they would ring as soon as I was in the recovery room. The call finally came at around 5:30 that evening, to say that I was OK but that I wouldn't be up to visitors until the following day.

I, of course, was blissfully unaware of the panic that I had caused. The operation had gone well and I was back in the recovery room by 10:45 a.m. Apparently I was starting to show signs of coming round, when I started to haemorrhage causing my heart to stop beating. I was rushed back into the theatre for a second operation, which of course was successful, or else I wouldn't be telling you my experience today.

While all the panic was taking place, I was in what I can only call a state of limbo. I felt extremely relaxed with not a care in the world and all I could see was a white mist. Then I felt something touch my bare shoulders and as I turned my eyes upwards, I could see an enormous pair of white, feathered wings. At that moment I felt safe and in my heart I knew my guardian angel was there to protect me.

I was reluctant to tell anyone of my apparition, because I felt they would probably think that I had gone a little potty! It has only been in recent years, when I have needed to call on my angel to protect other members of my family, that I have been brave enough to tell my story. To my amazement, instead of my friends and family laughing, they were in awe of my experience and said they wished they could have such a powerful belief.

I would definitely not call myself a superstitious person and keep an open mind about ghosts and supernatural beings.

However, having actually felt the presence of my guardian angel's wings brush my shoulders, I now know that I have someone there all the time who is taking care of me and my loved ones.

The command to love thy neighbour
embraces the holy angels also,
seeing that so great offices of
mercy have been performed
by them on our behalf.

Saint Augustine

VIRGINIA L

I have always believed in angels but never really focused on them.

I was living in a little cottage in Ojai, California and I was 33 or 34. I had a German Shepherd dog named Tanya. I had a neighbour who had two dogs but had to keep them apart because they were father and son and always fought. One day this neighbour wasn't there and the two dogs got into a fight and I had to separate them. The smaller, older dog was a bloody mess. I put him in my car as best I could and drove to the vet where they stitched him up. The bill was $50 and that was my Christmas spending money.

I came back to my little cottage and had my dog on one side of the bed and the neighbour's dog on the other side. I was exhausted and fell asleep. In the middle of the night, a beautiful blue light appeared to me and lifted me up and swung me around like a child. I felt so light and happy for a moment. When I woke up I wasn't sure what to make

of it. Then, later that afternoon, I was packing to go to Ohio for Christmas and felt bad that I had no money for Christmas gifts for my sister and mother. The doorbell rang and there was a UPS driver with a parcel. I didn't order anything, so I was puzzled by the delivery. There, beautifully wrapped were three different renditions of the house I grew up in painted by a family friend. She included a note apologising for taking so long to do these pictures, saying there would be no charge. (A year ago I had asked her to paint pictures of our family home for my sister and mother.) And now, here were my perfect Christmas presents. I learned a week or so later from a workshop I was attending that angels sometimes appear in the form of blue light.

This next story is pretty horrific, and was told to me by a youngish Hispanic woman who was in my modern dance class. I noticed that one side of her face was badly scarred and one of her eyes was half closed. She had two children and did sewing to supplement her income. I had her do lots of alterations to keep her going and one day asked her about her face and what had happened. It transpired that her ex-husband had been watching her kids at night so she could go to college for night classes. She took a bus, and the bus dropped her off fairly close to the college, but it was raining that night and a car slowed down and the driver asked her if he could take her to class. She thought she knew the guy from her class and accepted. The minute she got in she sensed a cold wave and thought 'oh oh!' Sure enough, he overpowered her and actually drove her back to Ojai where we have orchards. I think he raped her and then dumped her out of the car, but drove over her head with the car tyres so she wouldn't be able to recognise him. Because it had been raining her head was somehow sunk into the mud so she didn't die as he thought. He drove away and she said two angels in sort of a golden white light came up on either side of her and lifted her up under each arm and carefully flew her across the street and stood with her on someone's front porch. One of the angel's wings lifted her limp arm and helped her ring the doorbell. The wife answered the door and was horrified by what she saw. Her husband, who was a lawyer, called the ambulance and they rode with her to the hospital. I don't know if they ever caught the man who attacked her, but several doctors who heard her story have come forward to operate on her for free.

Isn't that a remarkable story!

My third story is not so exciting, but took place in Pasadena where I lived at the time taking care of my aunt. I had been reading a book called *The Messenger* by Julia Ingram about a man named Nick who discovered that he had walked alongside Jesus as Paul the Apostle. He also kept waking up at 4:44 am and didn't know what to make of it. Some of his business colleagues also woke at 4:44 and thought about him. His hypnosis

VIRGINIA L *(continued)*

sessions continued and eventually Nick left his life as a successful businessman to write a book about the truths in the Bible. He has a newsletter now and I actually went to hear him speak in the 1990s. Anyway I went to bed and had the thought 'I wonder if angels actually have wings and if they are actually made of feathers as depicted in drawings'. Right around early morning I felt the softest touch to my right cheek like a feather. When I woke up I knew the book had some sort of encoded energy and I had indeed been stroked by a feathered angel. Sometimes when I ask for a sign I'll see 444 on my speedometer or on a licence plate or wherever.

Author's note:

As described in his book, *In God's Truth*, starting in 1977, nine psychics and mystics in three different states independently told Nick Bunick that he was the soul who lived 2,000 years ago and was known as the Apostle Paul. Nick, who by now had become a successful businessman and who served on the boards of several corporations, found this premise difficult to accept.

Over the years, Nick himself started to receive telepathic messages from angelic beings, who he calls the 'messengers'. In the spring of 1996, at 4:44 in the morning, Nick was awakened by the messengers and told that a book about his being St Paul would be written and distributed in Seattle. 444 had become a symbol for Nick, as important events in his spiritual journey seemed to be associated with the number 444. The first half of the book is a narrative which summarises Nick's story and the second half consists of transcripts of past life regressions that Nick underwent conducted by Julia Ingram, a professional hypnotherapist, which began in 1991. In these regressions, Nick accessed memories of his past life as the Apostle Paul. Thousands of people have had '444 experiences', which Bunick has been told by 'spirit' is a symbol for the power of God's love.

NANCY McA

I have felt at two distinct times in my life that I had guardian angels. Once when I was very young (pre-kindergarten, I think) I came close to drowning at a friend's pool and I felt something or someone pull me to safety.

Another time, in middle school, I was on a runaway horse and, for some inexplicable reason, the horse turned and didn't go inside the barn where I would have surely been killed by a low-hanging beam.

I feel that angels are real, just as I know God and Jesus and the Holy Spirit are real. We can feel them, even if we don't see them. I was with both my parents when they died and I can attest to what hospice nurses always say – that heavenly bodies are present in the room.

If we were all angels, the world
would be a heavenly place.

Author unknown

NAMING ANGELS

Do angels have names? The practice of giving or assigning names to angels has been reviled by many religious sectors. Some churches have gone to great lengths to prevent this practice, with little success. While almost all religions openly acknowledge and accept the names mentioned in the Scriptures (Michael, Gabriel, Raphael, and Uriel), many have passed decrees against it.

The attributes of some of these higher-ranking angels are said to be:

Michael – protection, power and initiative
Gabriel – love, tolerance and gratitude
Raphael – healing, consecration and truth
Uriel – devotion, peace and ministration

There are many other 'named' angels that protect, inspire, assist and encourage. Some of these are:

Afriel – protector of children and young animals
Akriel – inspires intellectual achievements and improves memory and higher knowledge
Anahita – female angel who keeps the earth fruitful and fertile – the protector of those who are caretakers of nature
Anauel – angel of success, commerce and prosperity. Protects those who own or start their own business
Balthial – helps overcome feelings of jealousy and bitterness. Inspires contentment and peace of mind
Barbelo – female angel of abundance, goodness, faith and integrity
Camael – presides over beauty, joy, happiness and contentment. Helps bring out one's inner qualities
Cathetel – guardian of the garden. Increases growth and yield of vegetables and fruits
Elemeniah – watches over those who travel on the water
Enoch – helps with writing and expression. Brings out the ability of writing and is an inspiration of new ideas
Hatatah – inspires positive and loving thoughts and gives insight into mysteries and hidden knowledge
Harahel – protects libraries, archives and places of learning. Protects those who pursue knowledge
Hariel – in charge of protecting domestic animals

Israfel – the angel of music. Inspires singing, playing musical instruments and writing music

Liwet – presides over inventions. Protector of those who have original ideas and thoughts

Mihr – angel of platonic love, friendship and companionship

Mumiah – presides over longevity and can grant long life

Nemamiah – guardian of those who fight for good causes

Rhamiel – inspires one to become compassionate in life

Samandiriel – inspires creativity and vivid imagination. Helps to develop artistic, creative and imaginative abilities

Sandalphon – especially receptive to all prayers

Satarel – angel of hidden, elusive and secret knowledge

Zadkiel – a special angel of mercy

If this particular aspect of angelology interests you, you can research it on the internet.

With regard to naming your own personal angel, some religious people feel it is a sign of disrespect. But I think that naming your angel is a good idea since we want to develop a loving relationship with this being that will be with us forever. It is easier to have a relationship with someone whose name we know, so to ask your angel to reveal their name to you, or give them a name that you feel comfortable with, will help you be more aware of them and more open to their guidance.

I also find it very fascinating that there are so many names meaning 'angel', 'messenger' and the like. Conversely, there are many names that translate as 'destroyer' or 'angel of death'. They will not be discussed here as I cannot imagine anyone bestowing a name with dark connotations on anyone else.

Some of the more popular or interesting 'good angel' names are:

MALE

Ange – French word meaning 'angel', 'messenger'

Angelico – Italian form of Latin 'angelicus', meaning 'angelic'

Angelo – Italian form of Latin 'angelus' meaning 'angel, 'messenger'. There are Greek, Portuguese and Bulgarian variations of this.

Engel – short form of longer Germanic names containing the word 'engel', meaning 'angel'. Though the word 'engel' is the German word for the heavenly being, there are two other words which have often been confused with it so that names containing such words are difficult to translate. The first, 'Ingal', is an extended form of 'Ing', the name of the Old Norse fertility god. The second, 'Angel', is the old English spelling for 'Angle', the name of the Germanic tribe of the Jutland peninsula who invaded eastern and northern Britain in the 5th–6th centuries and gave their name to England. To further complicate matters, angel is also the Old English word for 'angle', which has fishing connotations in both English and German.

Engelbert – old German name probably composed of the elements 'engel' and 'berht' which means bright, famous, therefore 'bright angel'.

Gabriel – anglicised form of Greek Gabriēl (Hebrew Gabriyel), meaning 'man of God' or 'warrior of God'. This is the name of one of the seven archangels of religious lore. In the Bible, he is known as the Messenger Angel – one of the two highest-ranking angels – and apart from Michael is the only other angel given a name in the Old Testament where he is first mentioned in the Book of Daniel. He is the angel who announced the births of John the Baptist and Jesus. He is said to watch over Iran (Persia), and in Ezekiel's vision of the cherubim (the four sacred animals), the face of the eagle corresponds to him. In ancient astrology, he corresponds to the sign of Taurus and rules over the moon.

Michael – anglicised form of Greek Michaēl (Hebrew Miyka'el), meaning 'who is like God?' or literally 'El's likeness'. In the Old Testament, this is the name of many characters, including the prince of Angels, the first archangel who was closest to God and became the guardian angel of Israel. In the New Testament, he leads the angelic host against the apocalyptic dragon. The Dead Sea Scrolls contain a story entitled 'The War of the Sons of Light and the Sons of Darkness', in which Michael is described as the 'viceroy of heaven', a title said to once belong to Satan.

Michelangelo – Italian compound name composed of 'Michele' 'who is like God?' and 'Angelo' 'angel, messenger'.

Raphael – German, Portuguese and Spanish form of Hebrew 'Rephael' meaning 'healed of God' or 'whom God has healed'.

Uriel – anglicised form of Hebrew 'Uwriyel', meaning 'flame of God' or 'light of the Lord'. In the Bible, this is the name of a Levite, and the maternal grandfather of Abijah. It is also the name of one of the seven archangels whose names were removed from the Church's list of recognized angels in 145 A.D. Uriel was said to have been one of the angels stationed at God's throne. He was considered the wisest of the archangels because his light was not merely of the physical kind, but rather the ultra-spiritual kind, making him highly intellectually illuminated. Some think Uriel was the angel who warned Noah of the coming flood, and helped the prophet Ezra interpret a prediction concerning the coming Messiah. He is also said to be the angel of divine magic, alchemy, writing, earthquakes, floods, and other kinds of cataclysms.

FEMALE

Ange – English short form of Latin Angela, meaning 'angel, messenger'.

Angela – feminine form of Latin Angelus, meaning 'angel, messenger'.

Angelica – feminine form of Italian Angelico, meaning 'angelic'.

Angelina – diminutive form of Latin Angela, meaning 'little angel/messenger'.

Angie – English short form of Latin Angela, meaning 'angel, messenger'.

Evangeline – English literary name composed of the Greek elements eu 'good, well' and angeles 'angel, messenger', and the French diminutive suffix -ine, hence 'good little angel'. It is a feminine form of Latin Evangelus.

RECIPES

As angels are spirits they don't need sustenance and nourishment. So it might seem odd to you that angel recipes are included in this book. Are these dishes prepared by angels or for angels?

I've gathered a collection of recipes here that I think of as 'angel food' – delicate, light dishes such as might please an angel. There seems to be a preponderance of sweet offerings, which suggests that angels might have a sweet tooth.

If angels did eat and drink, they would probably like these and anyway they are certainly good for the soul!

'When one has tasted watermelon he knows what the angels eat.'

MARK TWAIN (SAMUEL LANGHORNE CLEMENS) (1835-1910)

Cocktails

Angel Punch

This is a gorgeous non-alcoholic punch that would be suitable for a large summer garden party.

Makes about 45 servings

YOU WILL NEED:
240 ml (8 fl oz) sugar syrup
480 ml (16 fl oz) lemon juice
900ml (1½ pints) strong green tea
2 litres (3½ pints) white grape juice
1 block of ice
2 litres (3½ pints) chilled soda water
Fresh flowers to decorate

1. Combine all ingredients except soda water, and refrigerate for an hour or two. Pour over ice in a punch bowl and add the soda water. Decorate with fresh flowers.

2. Serve in 120 ml (4 fl oz) punch glasses.

Blue Angel Cocktail

Cool, creamy and refreshing

Makes 2 servings

YOU WILL NEED:
60 ml (2 fl oz) brandy
30 ml (1 fl oz) blue curaçao
30 ml (1 fl oz) vanilla crème de cacao
30 ml (1 fl oz) single cream or half cream
Dash of lemon juice
Lemon slices to garnish

1 . In a cocktail mixer full of ice, combine the brandy, blue curaçao, crème de cacao, cream and lemon juice.

2. Shake vigorously and strain into two cocktail glasses.

3. Garnish with a slice of lemon.

Fallen Angel Cocktail

Serves 3-4

YOU WILL NEED:
150 ml (5 fl oz) gin
90 ml (3 fl oz) blue curaçao
60 ml (2 fl oz) freshly squeezed
   lemon juice
2 dashes Angostura bitters
Ice cubes
210 ml (7 fl oz) lemonade

1. Combine the gin, blue curaçao, lemon juice and bitters in a jug.

2. Divide amongst 3–4 glasses, add ice cubes and fill the glasses with lemonade.

Flaming Angel Cocktail

Makes 2 cocktails

YOU WILL NEED:
60 ml (2 fl oz) gin
Juice of 1 lemon
Juice of 1 lime
150 ml (5 fl oz) tonic water
2 dashes grenadine syrup

1. Fill a cocktail shaker with ice. Add the gin, lemon and lime juice and shake.

2. Strain the mixture into two cocktail glasses. Add the tonic water.

3. Drop a dash of grenadine syrup into each glass allowing it to sink to the bottom. The grenadine is the 'flame'.

Nutty Angel Cocktail

This may be called an 'angel' cocktail, but it's sinful enough to be dessert.

Serves 2

YOU WILL NEED:
60 ml (2 fl oz) vodka
60 ml (2 fl oz) hazelnut liqueur
60 ml (2 fl oz) Irish cream liqueur
30 ml (1 fl oz) crème de cacao
Nutmeg to dust

1. Put all the ingredients except the nutmeg into a cocktail shaker filled with ice.

2. Strain into two chilled martini glasses and dust with nutmeg.

3. Cheers!

Savouries

Angel and Devil Soup

A whimsical take on Chinese Hot and Sour soup.

Serves 4

YOU WILL NEED:

1 litre (1¾ pints) homemade or bought
    chicken stock
45 g (1½ oz) dried shiitake mushrooms
75 ml (2½ fl oz) rice vinegar
2 tablespoons cornflour
22 ml (¾ fl oz) toasted sesame oil
3 tablespoons finely chopped fresh ginger
280 g (10 oz) firm tofu, cut into small cubes
30 g (1 oz) bean thread noodles or angel hair
    pasta, broken in half
1 tablespoon soy sauce
½ teaspoon dried red chilli flakes
Pinch of sugar

1. Combine the stock and dried mushrooms in a bowl. Let stand until mushrooms soften, about 20 minutes. Remove mushrooms from the stock and squeeze dry over the bowl; reserve the stock.

2. Discard mushroom stems and thinly slice the caps.

3. Combine the vinegar and cornflour in a small bowl; stir to blend.

4. Heat the oil in a large saucepan over a high heat. Add the ginger and sauté for 30 seconds. Pour in the reserved stock. Bring to the boil. Add the tofu, noodles, soy sauce, red chilli flakes, sugar and mushrooms. Reduce the heat to medium-low, cover and simmer 5 minutes.

5. Add the cornflour mixture and stir until slightly thickened, about 1 minute. Serve hot.

Angels on Horseback

Makes 12

YOU WILL NEED:
12 shelled oysters
120 ml (4 fl oz) dry white wine
1 large garlic clove, finely chopped
Salt and freshly ground black pepper
6 rashers streaky bacon, cut in half

1. Put the oysters in a bowl. Add the wine, garlic, salt and pepper and mix to combine. Marinate for 15–20 minutes.

2. Preheat the grill to high. Wrap each oyster with a piece of bacon and secure with a cocktail stick. Place on a baking tray.

3. Grill on both sides until the bacon is crisp.

4. Serve immediately.

Avocado Angel Eggs

You've all probably encountered devilled eggs. These, originally from the California Avocado Commission, are their heavenly counterparts. As the story goes, a little five-year-old was in the kitchen watching his mother prepare canapés and asked what she was making. 'Devilled eggs', she said. 'The devil is evil' said the little boy. 'Can't you make angel eggs?' And so they have been in that household ever since.

Makes 24

YOU WILL NEED:
12 large hard boiled eggs, peeled
2 ripe avocados
1 tablespoon lemon juice
¼ teaspoon garlic powder
2 tablespoons chopped shallots
Salt and freshly ground white pepper to taste

1. Slice each egg in half, lengthways. Remove the yolks and either use for another recipe (sprinkled over cooked cauliflower, perhaps) or chop for this one.

2. Mash the avocado with the egg yolks, if using, lemon juice, garlic powder and shallots. Season with salt and white pepper.

3. Fill the egg whites with the avocado mixture and serve either at room temperature or chilled.

Angel Hair Pasta with Mussels

Serves 4

YOU WILL NEED:

225 g (8 oz) dried angel hair pasta
2 teaspoons olive oil
5 tablespoons chopped onion
3 cloves garlic, finely chopped
2 red peppers, seeded and diced
½ teaspoon salt
Pinch of red chilli flakes
400 g (14 oz) tin tomatoes, undrained and
    chopped
120 ml (4 fl oz) dry white wine
36 mussels (about 1.5 kg/3¼ lb), scrubbed
    and bearded
3 tablespoons chopped fresh parsley

1. Cook pasta according to packet instructions, omitting salt. Drain and keep warm.

2. Meanwhile, heat the oil in a large saucepan over a medium-high heat. Add the onion and garlic; sauté 5 minutes until tender.

3. Add the peppers, salt and red chilli flakes and sauté for 2 minutes.

4. Add the tomatoes and wine. Bring to the boil, reduce the heat to low and simmer 10 minutes.

5. Add the mussels. Increase the heat to medium. Cover the pan and simmer for 7 minutes or until shells open. Discard any mussels with unopened shells.

6. Serve the mussels over the pasta, sprinkled with the parsley.

Fiery Angels

Spicy bacon-wrapped prawns make an impressive first course.
This could also be a main course, served over rice.

Serves 4 as a starter, 2 as a main course

YOU WILL NEED:
450 g (1 lb) streaky bacon rashers
2 tablespoons onion powder
2 tablespoons dried oregano
2 tablespoons dried basil
1 tablespoon dried thyme
1 tablespoon freshly ground black pepper
1 teaspoon white pepper, or to taste
1 teaspoon cayenne pepper, or to taste
5 tablespoons paprika
450 g (1 lb) large prawns, peeled and de-veined

1. Cut the bacon rashers into thirds. In a large frying pan, sauté the bacon for 5 minutes until cooked, but not yet crisp.

2. In a bowl, combine the onion powder, oregano, basil, thyme, black pepper, white pepper, cayenne pepper and paprika. Taste the spice mix and if it isn't hot enough for your liking, add more black, white and cayenne pepper to taste.

3. Coat the prawns with the spices, either by dipping them into the bowl, or pouring the spices into a plastic bag and adding the prawns a few at a time and shaking.

4. Wrap the bacon around the prawns, securing them with a cocktail stick.

5. Sauté the prawns in the frying pan you used for the bacon over a medium heat until the bacon is crisp and the prawns are pink. Serve hot.

Angel Scones

Makes 24 scones

YOU WILL NEED:
7 g (¼ oz) sachet active dry yeast
60 ml (2 fl oz) warm water, 45°C (110°F)
550 g (1¼ lb) plain flour
55 g (2 oz) granulated sugar
1 teaspoon bicarbonate of soda
1 tablespoon baking powder
1½ teaspoons salt
480 ml (16 fl oz) buttermilk *or* soured milk*
225 g (8 oz) solid vegetable fat
30 g (1 oz) butter, melted

1. Dissolve yeast in the warm water.

2. Sift together flour, sugar, bicarbonate of soda, baking powder and salt. Add buttermilk and dissolved yeast. Blend in vegetable fat. Store dough, covered, in the refrigerator until ready to use.

3. Roll out on a lightly floured surface or shape into balls–these do not need to rise. Brush tops of scones with melted butter.

4. Preheat the oven to 200°C (400°F/Gas Mark 6).

5. Bake for 15–20 minutes until golden-brown.

n.b. Soured milk can be made by adding 15 g (1 tablespoon) lemon juice or vinegar to each 240 ml (8 fl oz) milk.

Angel Dinner Rolls

Makes 12–16

YOU WILL NEED:

7 g (¼ oz) sachet active dry yeast
60 ml (2 fl oz) tepid water (40°–46°C/
   105°–115°F)
280–350 g (10–12 oz) plain *or* bread flour
2 tablespoons sugar
1 teaspoon baking powder
½ teaspoon bicarbonate of soda
1 teaspoon salt
120 ml (4 fl oz) vegetable oil
240 ml (8 fl oz) buttermilk *or* soured milk
   (*see page 123*)
Additional butter to brush (optional)

1. Preheat oven to 180°C (350°F/Gas
Mark 4).

2. Dissolve the yeast in the tepid water in a
bowl. Allow to stand for 5 minutes until
frothy.

3. Combine the flour, sugar, baking powder,
bicarbonate of soda and salt in a large bowl.
Make a well in the centre.

4. Combine the oil, buttermilk and yeast
mixture. Add to dry ingredients, stirring until
just moistened. The dough will be sticky.

5. Turn the dough out onto a lightly floured
surface. Roll out to 1 cm (½-inch) thickness
and cut out circles with a 6.5 cm (2½-inch)
biscuit cutter.

6. Place the rolls on an ungreased baking tray,
brush with butter if desired and bake for
about 16 minutes, until golden-brown.

Angel Bread – Bread Machine Recipe

A light and heavenly bread that has a wonderful taste and a soft, fluffy texture. Make sure you grease your loaf tins and you will be rewarded with two delightful loaves of bread.
(Recipe provided by Angel S. who also had an angel encounter – see page 67.)

Makes 2 loaves

YOU WILL NEED:
240 ml (8 fl oz) water
1 large egg
1 teaspoon lemon juice
55 g (2 oz) butter, cut into small cubes
1 teaspoon salt
55 g (2 oz) granulated sugar
3 tablespoons powdered coffee creamer or
    dried milk (I use creamer)
2 tablespoons instant potato flakes
450 g (1 lb) bread flour
1 tablespoon bread machine yeast
Butter to brush

1. Grease two 900 g (2 lb) bread tins.

2. Add the ingredients in the order listed by your bread machine manufacturer.

3. Select the dough cycle and push start.

4. When the cycle is finished, remove the dough to a lightly floured board and cut in half.

5. Shape each half into a loaf and place in the greased tins. Cover and let rise until doubled in size (about 50–60 minutes).

6. Preheat the oven to 180°C (350°F/Gas Mark 4). Bake the loaves for 30 minutes.

7. Remove from the oven and brush the tops with butter.

8. Remove from the bread tins and cool on a wire rack.

9. When completely cool, store in plastic bags and freeze one loaf if you like. Enjoy!

Heavenly Cornbread

This is one of those recipes written on a scrap of paper that gets passed down from generation to generation. It is wonderful served with a chilli or a stew so that you can sop up the liquid.

Serves 4

YOU WILL NEED:
225 g (8 oz) maize meal
115 g (4 oz) plain flour
7 g (¼ oz) sachet active dry yeast
1 tablespoon sugar
1½ teaspoons baking powder
½ teaspoon bicarbonate of soda
1 teaspoon salt
2 eggs, beaten
480 ml (16 fl oz) buttermilk *or* soured milk
   (*see page 123*)
120 ml (4 fl oz) corn oil

1. Preheat the oven to 200°C (400°F/Gas Mark 6).

2. Combine the maize meal, flour, yeast, sugar, baking powder, bicarbonate of soda and salt in a bowl.

3. In a separate bowl combine the eggs, buttermilk and corn oil.

4. Mix the egg mixture into the flour mixture and blend well.

5. Grease a cast iron frying pan well. Pour the batter in and bake for 20–25 minutes until the edges are slightly brown and the centre is set.

6. Remove from the oven and cool slightly. Cut into wedges and serve with a chilli or a recipe of your choice.

You can also bake the cornbread in muffin tins, but you may need to decrease the baking time slightly, so just keep an eye on it.

Angel Breakfast Puff

This is a brilliant casserole that you can be creative with. Add bacon, ham or sausages for a more substantial dish. The great thing about it is everyone usually loves it and if you have breakfast guests, this is a very easy dish to serve. Just add some fruit and toast and voila! Easy breakfast for a crowd.

Serves 8–12

YOU WILL NEED:

12 eggs
225 g (8 oz) mature Cheddar cheese, grated
225 g (8 oz) Emmenthal or Gruyère cheese, grated
450 g (16 oz) curd cheese *or* cottage cheese
55 g (2 oz) plain flour
1 teaspoon baking powder
½ teaspoon salt
Freshly ground white pepper
115 g (4 oz) melted butter
Freshly chopped parsley to garnish

1. Preheat the oven to 180°C (350°F/Gas Mark 4).

2. In a large bowl, whisk the eggs until they are light and fluffy.

3. Add the three cheeses, flour, baking powder, salt, pepper and melted butter and mix until well blended.

4. Pour into a greased 23 x 33 cm (9 x 13-inch) baking dish and bake for 30 minutes.

5. Remove from the oven, sprinkle with parsley and serve immediately or keep warm.

Oriental Angel Noodles

Lovely comfort food, Asian style. Like a Chinese takeaway you make yourself.

Makes 2 servings

YOU WILL NEED:

225 g (8 oz) angel hair pasta
1 teaspoon rapeseed oil
1 teaspoon toasted sesame oil
Half an onion, chopped
1 clove garlic, finely chopped
1 skinless, boneless raw chicken breast, cut into bite-sized pieces
1 tablespoon grated fresh ginger
2 leaves pak choi, shredded
60 ml (2 fl oz) chicken stock
2 tablespoons dry sherry
1 tablespoon soy sauce
1½ tablespoons hoisin sauce
2 spring onions, finely chopped

1. Cook the angel hair pasta in plenty of boiling salted water until just *al dente*. Drain and keep warm.

2. Heat the oils in a large non-stick frying pan over a medium-high heat. Sauté the onion and garlic until softened. Add the chicken and cook until the chicken browns slightly and is just cooked. Stir in the ginger, pak choi, chicken stock, sherry, soy sauce and hoisin sauce. Reduce the heat and continue to cook for 10 minutes.

3. Toss the pasta with the chicken mixture. Serve warm, sprinkled with the reserved spring onions.

Sweets

Angelica

Angelica is a plant related to the parsley family. Of the many species growing in the temperate regions of the world, the most famous and useful is *Angelica archangelica.*

The basis for its angelic associations is not clear, although it might be connected with the plant's reputation as an antidote to poisons and the archangelic ones may be due to the fact that the flower would be in bloom on 8 May, the date commemorating the apparition of St Michael the Archangel in Italy in the year 492 AD.

A. archangelica grows well in the UK. Formerly the leaf stalks were blanched and eaten like celery and the leaves were crystallised. The roots were made into preserves and angelica water was a well-known cordial. Nowadays the most common use is to crystallise the stalks for use in desserts, cakes and confectionery.

If you have angelica growing in your garden, you might be interested in crystallising it yourself as it is so much nicer than the sort you buy in the shops.

YOU WILL NEED:
3–4 sprigs angelica, at least 2 years old
1 tablespoon bicarbonate of soda
225 g (8 oz) caster sugar
caster sugar, for sprinkling (optional)

1. Cut angelica stalks in their 2nd year. Unlike many other plants, large stalks are better as long as they are still green (not purple or white).

2. Remove the leaves, cut the stems into pieces about 15 cm (6 inches) long and soak in cold water overnight.

3. Boil 3.5 litres (6 pints) of water in a large saucepan. Add bicarbonate of soda to retain

the vivid green colour and help soften the angelica. Plunge the stalks in the boiling water to blanch them.

4. Make a syrup with the sugar and 240 ml (8 fl oz) water. Soak the stalks in this syrup for 24 hours.

5. Cook the angelica in this syrup for 20 minutes. Repeat once a day for 4 days, by which time the angelica should be translucent without losing its shape.

6. After you have repeated this four times, boil the angelica in the syrup again for 10 minutes, adding water if the syrup is too thick, and drain on a wire rack for 4 days longer.

7. Dust with caster sugar and store in an airtight container for up to one year, cutting into decorative bits as needed.

Angel Toast

Children will just love these for a special breakfast treat. They are also great for children's parties!

YOU WILL NEED:
Sliced white bread
Sweetened condensed milk
Flaked coconut
Chopped nuts (optional)

1. Preheat the oven to 180°C (350°F/Gas Mark 4).

2. Cut angel shapes from the sliced white bread with biscuit cutters.

3. Dip in condensed milk and sprinkle with flaked coconut and chopped nuts.

4. Grease a baking sheet or line with parchment paper and arrange the angel bread shapes on it. Bake for 10-15 minutes until golden.

Angel Salad

❧❧❧ ❀ ❧❧❧

This type of moulded salad is very popular in the US, especially in the Southern states. Sometimes it is made with fruit gelatine, but it has a nicer texture without.

Serves 4–6

YOU WILL NEED:

560 g (20 oz) tinned pineapple rings or chunks, drained and crushed
450 g (1 lb) mini marshmallows
225 g (8 oz) maraschino cherries, chopped
85 g (3 oz) cream cheese
2 tablespoons caster sugar
2 tablespoons mayonnaise
240 ml (8 fl oz) whipping or double cream, whipped
55 g (2 oz) pecans, halved or chopped
mint leaves to garnish

1. In a bowl, combine the pineapple and marshmallows.

2. In another bowl, mix the cherries, cream cheese, sugar and mayonnaise together. Add the whipped cream and fold in to combine.

3. Gently fold the cream mixture into the pineapples and marshmallows. Add the pecans.

4. Transfer to a glass bowl and chill until firm.

5. To serve, scoop into dessert glasses and garnish with mint leaves.

Angelberry Delight

When you are looking for a light dessert that takes very little effort and always gets compliments, try this.

Serves 8

YOU WILL NEED:

240 ml (8 fl oz) whipping cream
2 tablespoons caster sugar
450 g (1 lb) thick and creamy yogurt
20 cm (8-inch) angel food cake, bought or homemade, cut into 2.5 cm (1-inch) pieces
225 g (8 oz) fresh blueberries
225 g (8 oz) fresh raspberries
225 g (8 oz) fresh strawberries, cut into halves or quarters if large
Chocolate sauce to garnish (optional)

1. In a chilled bowl, whisk the whipping cream and sugar with an electric whisk on high speed until stiff peaks form. Gently fold in the yogurt.

2. Place the cake cubes in a large bowl. Fold in the yogurt mixture. Mix the berries together in another bowl.

3. Spoon half the cake mixture into a 23 cm (9-inch) springform cake tin. Press down firmly with a rubber spatula. Top with half of the berries. Repeat with the remaining cake, pressing down again with a spatula. Top with the remaining berries. Cover and refrigerate for at least 4 hours or overnight.

4. To serve, run a metal spatula carefully along the sides of the tin to loosen. Remove the side of the tin. Cut the dessert into wedges. Place on dessert plates and add a squiggle of chocolate sauce to decorate.

Cranberry Angel Whip

Makes 4 servings

YOU WILL NEED:
1 teaspoon unflavoured gelatine
2 tablespoons cold water
250 g (9 oz) cranberry sauce
4 tablespoons icing sugar
2 egg whites
120 ml (4 fl oz) double cream, whipped
½ teaspoon vanilla essence
Additional whipped cream or custard to serve

1. Soften the gelatine in the cold water.

2. Heat half the cranberry sauce in a saucepan and dissolve the gelatine. Cool the mixture, then add the icing sugar and remaining cranberry sauce.

3. Whisk the egg whites in a bowl until they hold stiff peaks. Fold into the cranberry mixture with the whipped cream and vanilla essence. Pour into a serving bowl and chill for several hours before serving with additional whipped cream or custard.

Naughty Angel Fondue

Orange liqueur and grated orange rind add a touch of elegance to this simple indulgence. Prepare the fondue just before serving and keep it warm so that it will remain smooth. Feel free to substitute other fruit-flavoured liqueurs such as Framboise or Fraise.

Serves 4

YOU WILL NEED:

75 ml (2½ fl oz) double cream

2 teaspoons grated orange rind

225 g (8 ounces) good quality plain chocolate, finely chopped

3 tablespoons orange liqueur or liqueur of your choice

8 cubes madeira cake

8 cubes angel food cake

8 fresh strawberries

2 kiwis, peeled, each cut into 4 rounds

1 small ripe pear, cored, cut into cubes

1 large ripe banana, cut into rounds

1 orange, peeled and cut into segments

8 dried figs

8 dried apricots

1. Bring cream and grated orange rind to the simmer in a heavy medium saucepan. Reduce the heat to low.

2. Add the chopped chocolate and 15 ml (1 tablespoon) of the orange liqueur; whisk until the mixture is smooth. Remove the chocolate fondue from the heat and blend in remaining liqueur.

3. Put the fondue into a heatproof bowl and keep warm. Arrange the cake and fruits on a serving plate and serve with fondue forks or skewers to dip.

Angel Kisses (Forgotten Cookies)

These are gorgeous, melt in the mouth meringues, given a bit of interest by the chocolate chips and pecans. They are usually called forgotten cookies because you leave them in the oven overnight.

Makes about 24 biscuits

YOU WILL NEED:
2 large egg whites
Pinch of salt
140 g (5 oz) caster sugar
½ teaspoon vanilla essence
170 g (6 oz) plain chocolate chips
115 g (4 oz) chopped pecans

1. Preheat the oven to 180°C (350°F/Gas Mark 4).

2. In a bowl, whisk the egg whites and salt until soft peaks form. Fold in the sugar and vanilla essence and continue whisking until stiff. Fold in the chocolate chips and pecans.

3. Line two baking sheets with parchment paper and drop the meringue mixture onto the trays with a teaspoon, 5 cm (2 inches) apart.

4. Put the baking sheets in the oven, immediately turn the heat off and leave the meringues in the oven without opening the door for at least 2 hours or overnight.

Angel Snack Bars

This is one of those recipes that are difficult to describe: these bars are salty, sweet, peanut buttery, chocolatey and so good, they are deadly because you just can't eat only one.
Best of all, you don't even have to bake them!

Makes 36 bars

YOU WILL NEED:
225 g (8 oz) plain biscuits, such as cream
    crackers, water biscuits, etc.
225 g (8 oz) salted butter
225 g (8 oz) soft brown sugar
5 tablespoons caster sugar
120 ml (4 fl oz) milk
115 g (4 oz) finely ground digestive
    biscuit crumbs
150 g (5½ oz) peanut butter
85 g (3 oz) milk chocolate chips
85 g (3 oz) plain chocolate chips

1. Line a 23 x 33 cm (9 x 13-inch) baking tin with aluminium foil. Spray the foil with non-stick vegetable oil spray. Place one layer of plain biscuits side by side in the tin without overlap.

2. Melt the butter in a small saucepan. Add the sugars and milk. Bring to the boil over a medium heat; reduce heat and simmer for 5 minutes. Add the digestive crumbs. Bring to the boil again and boil for 1 minute.

3. Spread half the digestive biscuit mixture over the biscuits in the baking tin. Place another layer of plain biscuits in the tin and spread evenly with the remaining digestive mixture. Top with a third layer of plain biscuits.

4. Put the peanut butter and chocolate chips in a microwaveable bowl and melt together in a microwave oven. Spread this mixture evenly over the top of the biscuits. Allow to cool, then chill in the refrigerator for at least 4 hours.

5. To serve, peel away the aluminium foil and cut into squares with a sharp knife. Serve as a snack or after dinner with coffee or tea.

Angel Cookies

This recipe was originally in a Minnesota farm journal many years ago.
The cookies are crunchy and wonderful.

Makes 4-5 dozen cookies

YOU WILL NEED:
115 g (4 oz) caster sugar
115 g (4 oz) soft brown sugar
225 g (8 oz) butter or margarine
1 egg, beaten
1 teaspoon vanilla essence
225 g (8 oz) plain flour
1 teaspoon bicarbonate of soda
1 teaspoon cream of tartar
Pinch of salt
Additional caster sugar to dip

1 . Preheat the oven to 180°C (350°F/Gas Mark 4).

2. Cream together the two sugars and butter or margarine. Add the egg and vanilla essence and beat well.

3. Stir in the flour, bicarbonate of soda, cream of tartar and salt. Roll into balls, dip top in water, then into sugar.

4. Place on ungreased parchment lined baking sheets. Flatten the cookies slightly. Bake for 8-10 minutes. Cookies will be pale, with just a tinge of colour at the edges. Remove from the oven and cool on wire racks.

Angel Whispers

These are little lemony sandwich biscuits that just melt in your mouth.
Have a few with a cup of tea or coffee.

Makes 24 biscuits

YOU WILL NEED:
For the biscuits:
225 g (8 oz) butter
55 g (2 oz) icing sugar
1 teaspoon lemon rind
225 g (8 oz) plain flour
½ teaspoon salt

For the filling:
1 egg, beaten
140 g (5 oz) granulated sugar
1½ teaspoons lemon rind
3 tablespoons lemon juice
45 g (1½ oz) butter

1. In a medium bowl cream together the butter and icing sugar until light. Stir in the lemon rind, flour and salt. Cover the bowl and chill for about one hour.

2. Preheat oven to 200°C (400°F/Gas Mark 6).

3. Place teaspoons of dough onto parchment-lined baking sheets, flatten and bake for 5–8 minutes, until golden brown. Remove biscuits from baking sheets to wire racks to cool completely.

4. To make the filling, combine the beaten egg, sugar, lemon rind, lemon juice and butter in the top of a double boiler. Heat, stirring until thick. Sandwich biscuits together with 1 teaspoon of filling.

Angel Pillows

*Soft and moist biscuits made with apricot jam. Peach jam is also a possibility.
Other nuts, such as walnuts or hazelnuts, can be substituted for the pecans if you prefer.*

Makes 18 biscuits

YOU WILL NEED:
For the biscuits:
115 g (4 oz) butter or margarine
85 g (3 oz) cream cheese, softened
1 tablespoon milk
55 g (2 oz) brown sugar
4 tablespoons apricot jam
140 g (5 oz) plain flour
1½ teaspoons baking powder
1½ teaspoons ground cinnamon
¼ teaspoon salt
55 g (2 oz) chopped pecans

For the icing:
115 g (4 oz) icing sugar
4 tablespoons apricot jam
1 tablespoon melted butter or margarine
4 tablespoons flaked coconut (optional)

1. Preheat the oven to 180°C (350°F/Gas Mark 4).

2. Make the biscuit dough. Grease baking sheets or line with parchment paper. In a medium bowl, cream together the butter or margarine, cream cheese and milk until well blended. Stir in the brown sugar and apricot jam. Combine the flour, baking powder, cinnamon and salt; stir into the batter. Mix in the pecans. Drop by rounded spoonfuls onto the prepared sheets. Biscuits should be about 5 cm (2 inches) apart.

3. Bake for 8–10 minutes in the preheated oven. Allow biscuits to cool on the baking sheet for five minutes before removing to a wire rack to cool completely.

4. To make the icing, combine the icing sugar, remaining apricot jam and melted butter or margarine; mix well. Ice the cooled biscuits and sprinkle with coconut if desired.

Polish Angel Wings

Makes 50–60 biscuits

YOU WILL NEED:
4 egg yolks, plus 1 whole egg
½ teaspoon salt
5 tablespoons icing sugar
2 tablespoons rum or brandy
1 teaspoon vanilla essence
140 g (5 oz) plain flour
750 ml (1¼ pints) vegetable oil for frying
Icing sugar for dusting

1. In the large bowl of an electric mixer combine the egg yolks, egg and salt. Beat on the highest speed until mixture is thick and drops softly from the beaters, 7–10 minutes.

2. Beat in the sugar, a small amount at a time. Beat in the rum or brandy and vanilla essence. Remove the bowl from the mixer.

3. Fold the flour into the mixture by hand until incorporated.

4. Turn the dough onto a generously floured work surface. Knead until blisters form on the dough, about 10 minutes. Add small amounts of flour as needed to keep dough from sticking. Divide dough in half. Cover one half with an inverted bowl, towel or clingfilm to prevent drying.

5. Roll out the other half of dough as thinly as possible into a 20 x 30 cm (8 x 12-inch) rectangle. If the dough resists, let it rest for a few minutes then resume rolling.

6. Cut dough into 5 x 10 cm (2 x 4-inch) rectangles. Make a 5 cm (2 inch) slit from the centre almost to the end of each dough strip. Pull the opposite end of strip through the slit to twist the dough. Repeat with remaining dough.

7. In a large frying pan heat the vegetable oil until it reaches 180°C (350°F) on a deep-fat thermometer. (This is important, if the oil is too cool, dough will absorb too much oil; if it is too hot, the pastry will burn on the outside and not cook properly on the inside.)

8. Add a few angel wings at a time and fry until golden on both sides, turning about halfway through the cooking time, about 1½ minutes total. Drain on kitchen paper. Repeat with the remaining angel wings. Cool completely and dust liberally with icing sugar. Store in airtight container for up to 1 week.

....

Anyone can be an angel.

AUTHOR UNKNOWN

....

Gingerbread Angels

When it comes to gingerbread, I almost always find that the allspice and cloves overpower the ginger flavour. To remedy that imbalance, I created a cookie with a double dose of ginger (ground and crystallised) and a little bit of cinnamon. And although the traditional cut for gingerbread is fat, sturdy men, I thought the lightness of angel wings seemed more appropriate for these delicate biscuits.

Makes 72

YOU WILL NEED:

675 g (1½ lb) plain flour
1 tablespoon ground ginger
1 tablespoon ground cinnamon
2 teaspoons bicarbonate of soda
1 teaspoon salt
85 g (3 oz) coarsely chopped crystallised ginger
225 g (8 oz) unsalted butter, room temperature
225 g (8 oz) caster sugar
100 g (3½ oz) light brown sugar
2 large eggs
60 ml (2 fl oz) golden syrup
60 ml (2 fl oz) fresh orange juice
2 teaspoons finely grated orange rind
1 egg white, beaten with 1 tablespoon water (optional, for glaze)
Coloured sugar to decorate (optional)

1. Sift the flour, ground ginger, cinnamon, bicarbonate of soda and salt in a large bowl.

2. Place the crystallised ginger in a small food processor or coffee grinder that you use for spices; add 15 ml (1 tablespoon) of the flour mixture and blend until the ginger is very finely chopped.

3. Using an electric mixer, beat the butter in another large bowl until smooth. Add the caster sugar and brown sugar; beat until light and fluffy. Whisk in the eggs, one at a time. Beat in the golden syrup, orange juice, and orange rind (the batter may look curdled). Beat in the crystallised ginger mixture. Blend in the remaining flour mixture. Gather the dough together and flatten into a disk. Wrap in clingfilm and chill for at least 4 hours.

4. Position one rack in the top third and one rack in the bottom third of the oven; preheat to 180°C (350°F/Gas Mark 4).

5. Line two baking sheets with parchment paper. Divide the dough into four portions and shape each into a round disk. Chill three of the disks. Roll out the remaining dough on a lightly floured work surface to 4 mm (generous ⅛-inch) thickness. Using a floured angel-shaped biscuit cutter, cut out the biscuits.

6. Gather the dough scraps and re-roll, then cut out more biscuits. Using a spatula, transfer the biscuits to the baking sheets, spacing them 2 cm (1 inch) apart. Brush them with glaze, then sprinkle with coloured sugar, if using.

7. Bake biscuits until golden, reversing sheets after 7 minutes, about 14 minutes total. Let stand for 2 minutes then transfer to wire racks to cool. Repeat with remaining dough, cooling the baking sheets between batches.

n.b. Can be made 1 week ahead. Store between sheets of parchment paper in an airtight container.

Adapted from a recipe by Damon Lee Fowler, *Bon Appetit*, December 2008

Ethereal Pumpkin Pie

This is the lightest and most delicious pumpkin pie you will ever try.
It has won over people who don't even like pumpkin!

Serves 8

YOU WILL NEED:

1 tablespoon unflavoured gelatine
120 ml (4 fl oz) cold water
4 large eggs, separated
240 ml (8 fl oz) evaporated milk
225 g (8 oz) pumpkin purée, bought or homemade
175 g (6 oz) soft brown sugar, divided
½ teaspoon salt
½ teaspoon grated nutmeg
½ teaspoon ground cinnamon
¼ teaspoon ground ginger
23 cm (9-inch) baked pastry case, bought or homemade
450 ml (15 fl oz) whipping cream, whipped with the reserved sugar

1. In a small bowl soften the gelatine in the cold water. Set aside.

2. In the top of a double boiler heat the egg yolks, evaporated milk, pumpkin, 115 g (4 oz) of the brown sugar (reserve the remainder to sweeten the cream), salt, nutmeg, cinnamon and ginger. Stir and cook gently for 10 minutes. Remove from the heat and mix in the gelatine, stirring until it is dissolved.

3. Chill the pumpkin filling until thick.

4. Whisk the egg whites until stiff. Fold into the chilled pumpkin mixture with a spatula.

5. Spoon the filling into the baked pastry case. Top with the sweetened whipped cream and refrigerate until ready to serve.

Angelic Molasses Cake

Sometimes it's good to have a cake that doesn't need to be iced.
This one is heavenly and delicious just as it is.

Makes one 20 cm (8-inch) square cake

YOU WILL NEED:
85 g (3 oz) butter or margarine
115 g (4 oz) caster sugar
115 g (4 oz) molasses *or* treacle
2 eggs, well beaten
120 ml (4 fl oz) buttermilk *or* soured milk
 (*see page 123*)
200 g (7 oz) plain flour, sifted twice
4 tablespoons cornflour
1 teaspoon bicarbonate of soda
1 teaspoon ground ginger
½ teaspoon salt

1. Preheat the oven to 180°C (350°F/Gas Mark 4).

2. Whisk the butter or margarine with an electric whisk. Add the sugar gradually and whisk thoroughly.

3. Add the molasses or treacle, eggs and milk and whisk again to combine.

4. Mix the flour, cornflour, bicarbonate of soda, ginger and salt together in a bowl and then add to the molasses mixture. Blend together well.

5. Pour into a greased 20 cm (8-inch) square tin and bake for 35–40 minutes until a skewer inserted near the centre comes out clean.

6. Remove from the oven and cool on a wire rack. When cold, cut into squares.

Lemon Angel Pie

Cream of tartar stabilises and adds volume to egg whites.

Serves 8–10

YOU WILL NEED:
4 egg whites, room temperature
¼ teaspoon cream of tartar
300 g (10½ oz) caster sugar, divided
4 egg yolks
75 ml (2½ fl oz) lemon juice
2 egg whites
480 ml (16 fl oz) whipping cream
1 tablespoon icing sugar
1 tablespoon lemon rind

A baby is an angel whose wings decrease as his legs increase.

AUTHOR UNKNOWN

1. Preheat the oven to 150°C (300°F/Gas Mark 2). Grease a 23 cm (9 inch) glass pie dish.

2. In a large bowl, whisk 4 egg whites with the cream of tartar until soft peaks form. Add 225 g (8 oz) sugar gradually, whisking until the mixture is stiff and glossy. Spread the meringue into the pie dish, making a well in the centre for the filling.

3. Bake for 1 hour. Turn off the oven, but do not open the door and leave the meringue in the oven for at least one hour or preferably overnight.

4. In a small, heavy saucepan, whisk together the egg yolks, lemon juice and remaining 75 g (2½ oz) sugar. Heat over a medium low heat until the mixture thickens and starts to bubble. Remove from the heat and transfer to a large bowl. Cover with clingfilm and allow to cool to room temperature.

5. In a small bowl whisk the 2 egg whites until stiff. Whip half the cream in another bowl. Fold the egg whites into the lemon mixture, then fold in the cream. Spread into the prepared meringue shell and cover with clingfilm. Chill for several hours.

6. When ready to serve, whip the remaining cream with the icing sugar and spoon over the top of the pie. Sprinkle with the lemon rind. This pie is best served on the day it is made.

Rhubarb Angel Dessert

A sort of pie with a shortbread crust, filled with rhubarb and topped with coconut meringue makes a heavenly dessert.

Serves 8–10

YOU WILL NEED:
For the crust:
115 g (4 oz) plain flour
1 tablespoon caster sugar
115 g (4 oz) cold butter, cut into small cubes

For the filling:
225 g (8 oz) caster sugar
2 tablespoons flour
¼ teaspoon salt
120 ml (4 fl oz) double cream
3 large egg yolks
450 g (1 lb) fresh rhubarb, chopped

For the meringue:
3 egg whites
85 g (3 oz) caster sugar
1 teaspoon vanilla essence
4 tablespoons toasted flaked coconut

1. Preheat the oven to 180°C (350°F/Gas Mark 4).

2. In a large bowl combine the flour and sugar. Cut in the butter until the mixture resembles coarse breadcrumbs.

3. Press the crust into an ungreased 20 cm (8-inch) square baking dish and bake in the preheated oven for 15–20 minutes until lightly browned. Remove from the oven.

4. Meanwhile, in a bowl combine the sugar, flour and salt. Whisk in the cream and egg yolks. Stir in the rhubarb. Pour over the hot crust. Bake, uncovered, for 40 minutes until set.

5. In a clean bowl whisk the egg whites, sugar and vanilla essence until soft peaks form. Spread over the rhubarb filling, ensuring that it is covered by the meringue. Bake for 15 minutes, until golden brown. Remove from the oven and sprinkle with the coconut. Cool on a wire rack.

6. To serve, cut into squares. Cover and refrigerate any leftovers.

How wonderful it must be to speak the language of the angels, with no words for hate and a million words for love!

QUOTED IN *THE ANGELS' LITTLE INSTRUCTION BOOK* BY EILEEN ELIAS FREEMAN, 1994

Angel Food Cake

This is a great way to use up excess egg whites and my friend Kathryn's favourite choice for her birthday cake. It has a wonderful texture and delicate flavour and is a terrific accompaniment for fresh fruit or ice cream.

Makes 8–10 servings

YOU WILL NEED:

100 g (3½ oz) sifted plain flour

1 tablespoon cornflour

375 g (13 oz) caster sugar, divided

420 ml (14 fl oz) egg whites (from about 12–13 large eggs)

½ teaspoon salt

1 teaspoon cream of tartar

½ teaspoon vanilla essence

For the glaze:

115 g (4 oz) sifted icing sugar

2 tablespoons lemon juice

1. Preheat the oven to 150°C (300°F/Gas Mark 2).

2. Sift the flour together with the cornflour three times, then sift this mixture with 140 g (5 oz) of the sugar.

3. Whisk the egg whites in a large bowl with an electric mixer at medium high speed until frothy. Add the salt and cream of tartar and whisk again until the whites just form soft peaks. Whisk in the remaining sugar a couple of tablespoons at a time. Add the vanilla essence and whisk again until the whites hold soft peaks.

4. Sift one quarter of the flour mixture over the whites and fold in gently, but thoroughly, then add the remaining flour in small amounts in the same way.

5. Spoon the mixture into an ungreased 25 cm (10-inch) tube tin and smooth the top. Tap on a counter top to eliminate any air bubbles.

6. Bake until the cake springs back when touched with a finger and a wooden skewer inserted near the centre comes out clean, about 75 minutes.

7. Remove from the oven. If the tin has feet, invert on a rack. If not, invert over the neck of a long-necked bottle. Cool for 2 hours.

8. Make the glaze. Sift the icing sugar into a bowl and mix with the lemon juice until smooth.

9. When you are ready to take the cake out of the tin, slowly run a long thin knife around the edges of the pan and the tube. Top with a rack and invert. Place a piece of parchment paper under the rack, pour the glaze over and leave to set.

10. Serve with fresh fruit or ice cream.

Chocolate Angel Food Cake

A not too naughty but luscious ethereal dessert.

Serves 12

YOU WILL NEED:

4 tablespoons unsweetened cocoa powder
60 ml (2 fl oz) boiling water
2 teaspoons vanilla essence
350 grams (12 oz) caster sugar
115 grams (4 oz) plain flour, sifted
¼ teaspoon salt
16 large egg whites (480 ml/16 fl oz) at room temperature
2 teaspoons cream of tartar

1. Preheat the oven to 180°C (350°F/Gas Mark 4) and place the oven rack in the centre of the oven.

2. In a small bowl, combine the cocoa powder and boiling water and stir until smooth. Add the vanilla essence and stir to combine.

3. In another bowl, mix together half the sugar, the sifted flour and the salt. Set aside.

4. In a large mixing bowl, whisk the egg whites with an electric whisk until foamy. Add the cream of tartar and continue to whisk until soft peaks form. Gradually whisk in the remaining sugar until stiff peaks form.

5. Remove a cupful of the whisked egg whites and fold it into the cocoa powder mixture.

6. Gradually sift the flour mixture over the egg whites and fold in gently, but thoroughly. Once the flour is incorporated into the egg whites, fold in the cocoa mixture. Do not overmix.

7. Pour the batter into a 25 cm (10 inch) tube tin (it will be almost full) and run a knife through the batter to get rid of any air pockets. Smooth the top with the knife and bake for 40-45 minutes, until the cake springs back when gently pressed. (There will be cracks in the top of the cake.)

8. Remove the cake from the oven and immediately invert the tin over the top of a wine bottle or similar. Allow to cool in this position for about 2 hours.

9. When completely cool, carefully run a knife around the sides and centre of the tin to loosen the cake and invert onto a rack. Now run the knife around the bottom of the tin and invert onto a serving plate. The cake will now be right side up.

10. Store covered for up to a few days at room temperature or up to a week in the refrigerator.

11. When ready to serve, dust with cocoa powder mixed with a bit of icing sugar or leave plain and serve with berries or fruit coulis and ice cream.

Chocolate Angel Torte

This is a tender angel cake with creamy almond filling.

Makes one 900 g (2 lb) loaf cake

YOU WILL NEED:

For the cake:

5 tablespoons sifted plain flour

3 tablespoons unsweetened cocoa powder

4 tablespoons caster sugar

6 egg whites

½ teaspoon salt

½ teaspoon cream of tartar

115 g (4 oz) caster sugar

1 teaspoon vanilla essence

For the filling:

4 tablespoons caster sugar

5 teaspoons cornflour

¼ teaspoon salt

2 eggs, beaten

240 ml (8 fl oz) milk

2 tablespoons almond liqueur

Sifted icing sugar to dust

1. Preheat the oven to 190°C (375°F/Gas Mark 5).

2. In a bowl sift the flour, cocoa powder and 4 tablespoons of caster sugar together.

3. In another bowl whisk the egg whites with the cream of tartar and salt until soft peaks form. Gradually add 115 g (4 oz) sugar, whisking until stiff and shiny, then add the vanilla essence. Sift the dry mixture over the whisked egg whites gradually and gently fold in. Spoon batter into a 900 g (2 lb) ungreased loaf tin.

4. Bake for 25 minutes until done.

5. Meanwhile, make the almond filling. Combine the sugar, cornflour and salt in a saucepan. Mix the beaten eggs and milk together and stir them into the sugar mixture. Cook over a medium heat, stirring constantly until thick and bubbling. Cook for an additional 2 minutes. Remove from the heat and add the almond liqueur and stir well. Cover the surface of the filling with clingfilm and chill completely before using.

6. When the cake is baked, remove from the oven, invert the tin onto a wire rack and cool completely. Remove the cake from the tin and cut it into 3 layers. Spread almond filling between the layers and dust the top with sifted icing sugar.

PICTURE ACKNOWLEDGEMENTS:

We would like to thank the following people for their kind permission to recreate their artwork:

ERVENE BOYD is a multi-media artist who lives in her home town of Raleigh, North Carolina. Her art is on permanent display at Namaste Holistic Wellness Center in Emerald Isle, NC and The University of North Carolina Women's Hospital in Chapel Hill, NC. Currently she has a 20-piece exhibition at Studio18 Salon in Cary, NC. Her artistic philosophy is a reflection of her holistic perspective. Diversity is the common thread in her life and work. She writes poetry, teaches Reiki, consults and practises various healing techniques. As a healing minister, ordained in the Order of Melchizedek since 1993, she officiates weddings and has a website, www.ervene.com.

MARIANNE HUNTER studied woven textiles at art school, and now lives and works in Kent. She has enjoyed painting angels by commission for the last eight years, and gains her inspiration through meditation. Contact moomoolouise@hotmail.com.

Third generation artist RENEE FAURE is the daughter of nationally recognised painter Nan Greacen Faure and granddaughter of prominent American impressionist Edmund W. Greacen. She is a member of the American Watercolor Society and a recently elected associate of the National Academy. She has exhibited and received awards on the national level with the American Watercolor Society, the National Watercolor Society and the National Society of Illustrators, among others. Her work has been published in the *National Society of Illustrators Annuals*, Volumes 18, 19, 28, and 29; the *Communication Arts 1980 Art Annual; North Light* magazine; *American Artist* magazine, feature article June 1982; and the book *Splash II*, 1992. Ms. Faure's paintings are included in numerous private and corporate collections around the US. Her current subject matter is predominantly the French countryside, and she has mounted three successful solo exhibitions on this theme over the past seven years. Five of these paintings have been reproduced in poster form by Bruce McGaw Graphics in New York and three others by Portal Publications in California.